Consumer Culture Is Consuming Us

By Michael Gold

This book is dedicated to Xiuhtezcatl Martinez, Anna Lee Rain Yellowhammer and Hallie Turner.

Consumer Culture Is Consuming Us

Consumer culture is killing our environment and destroying our humanity.

We live in a culture drenched in consumerism. It blares out messages by the minute to buy more and more goods to satisfy our constant, gnawing child-like wants right at this minute (which this culture helped create), from spicy tortilla chips and peanut butter chocolate bars to monster trucks and mini-mansions swollen with junk products masquerading as fulfillment for our souls. Corporations sell us lies and call them dreams.

Consumer culture has instructed us to regard our selfish wants in the highest esteem, to the exclusion of all other values. The United States is the leader in consumerism. We created it. We nurture it and we send it around the world and it is bringing us to our knees.

In a country where the vast hordes of consumers have been mobilized to lust after products to swallow whole, (people we used to call citizens), there is little room for a higher purpose among any of us. We value getting more stuff over anything else, including saving the environment which we depend on for life. Consumer culture tells us we should get whatever we want, right now. And once we get it, we should get more. We deserve it. And who cares about the consequences? That's somebody else's problem.

In the chapters that follow, I will write about this cancerous culture of manipulating us to seek instant gratification, which dominates virtually every part of our national life, including advertising, the mother that gave birth to this sickness, its hand-maiden -- entertainment, music, the beauty and body-building industries, gambling, lotteries, eating habits, the environment, politics, business, transportation, guns, and on and on, woven through virtually every human interaction we are capable of experiencing.

In later chapters I will discuss how to fight against this culture and reject it in order to live free of the pernicious influence of the diseased and depraved values that have left many of us emotional cripples unable to recognize what should matter the most in our lives.

This is not an exhaustive survey of the massive problem we face, but I hope it gets across my point that the lies the consumer culture propagates daily are harming our bodies, our relationships and the ability of human beings to live on this planet, our collective home.

Advertising –
Eating and Drinking

If Hollywood is the dream factory, then advertising is the dream machine.

If you buy a bottle or can of Coca Cola, you are not just buying a drink filled with carbonated water, high fructose corn syrup, caramel color, phosphoric acid, natural flavors (whatever that means) and caffeine. You are buying fun, laughs, friendship, romance, sex, wild music, adventure and a general delight in life. Coca Cola will make you enjoy life more. It will make you happy. It will be part of your great life, running on the beach, throwing snowballs, meeting a new boyfriend or girlfriend, sharing your latest news on your IPhone.

Pepsi Cola will free you to dance with total strangers on the New York City subway. Drinking Pepsi will make you bop to a Pepsi beat. It will make you sing at a diner, with someone of another skin color (Pepsi, can bring white and black people together and help end racism!). Pepsi can make cars in a traffic jam spring up and down because they are so happy from drinking Pepsi. Pepsi can interrupt a game of dominoes with a man's bouncing knee, a man so happy from drinking Pepsi that he pumps his leg up and down and bumps the table.

For a can filled with carbonated water, high fructose corn syrup, caramel color, natural flavors (What are these natural flavors, I'd like to know.), phosphoric acid, sodium citrate, caffeine, potassium sorbate (to preserve freshness), aspartame, citric acid, acesulfame potassium, sucralose and phenylalanine, this is amazing. You buy this product; you get joy in a can. Who wouldn't want that?

What the soda companies have done is absolute genius. They have inserted and integrated their products into everyday life. These cans of sugar and water are shown to be indispensable to daily living, whether you are at work or play. They are not just a mixture of brown water, chemicals and sugar, they are inspiration, they are pure undiluted happiness. They are present in the greatest emotional moments of your life.

Pretending to fulfill our dreams with soda comes at great cost.

The obesity epidemic has been fueled in part by our soda consumption and covered in great depth by the media. Medicaldaily.com, states that soda can help dissolve your tooth enamel, increase your chances of getting diabetes, and cause kidney and heart problems and a host of other medical issues. For a full discussion of soda's effect on your body, go to: medicaldaily.com.

Clearly, these poor health outcomes that may be caused by drinking soda are the exact opposite of the messages of youth, vigor and energy that the soda companies are saturating us with every day. The dreams they manufacture in order to compel us to buy their products are demented and outrageous lies.

It gets worse, because even if you don't drink soda, you will suffer the effects of the making of this product. When people finish drinking a can or bottle of soda, what do they do with it? Most soda consumers either throw it in the trash or in the streets. That's bad for everybody.

"More than 100 billion aluminum cans are sold in the United States each year, but less than half are recycled," according to Larry West, an environmental expert writing for aboutnews.com. That's 50 billion cans of carbon pollution. Overseas, it's the same story – about 50 billion cans are tossed away, to be incinerated or put in a landfill.

"Recycling one aluminum can save enough energy to run a TV for three hours -- or the equivalent of a half a gallon of gasoline," according to the Recycling R2evolution web site.

Who wants to recycle a can when you are living out your dreams from that can? The truth is, once you are done with the can, your dream is over, if it ever existed. It's easier to toss it in the grass than bother with the reality of what you have just consumed, which is essentially nothing.

Even water, that most basic of products, can provide you with these same joys. Commercials for Dasani (a Coca

Cola company product) shows how healthy it is. It shows people drinking Dasani and surfing, doing yoga or riding on a boat. The commercials say Dasani will keep your body pure. It has no sugar and no calories. Never mind that you can get the same benefits from drinking tap water.

Bottled water is everywhere. A Dasani commercial says the plastic is recyclable. Thirty percent is made from plants, according to the commercial. This is paraded out as if this was an incredibly big deal. OK, fine. That's better than what we had previously. But, what about the other 70 percent of the bottle? It's made from oil.

It takes about 17 million barrels of oil every year to make plastic water bottles, according to the Pacific Institute, a global water think tank. This is the equivalent of fueling one million cars for an entire year, the institute says.

It takes about four ounces of oil to make a 16-ounce bottle of water. (source: http://greenanswers.com).

And most people throw it away.

"Of the 30 billion plastic water bottles sold in the United States in 2005, only 12 percent were recycled," according to the Business Insider website.

Doug James, a professor of computer science and computer graphics at Cornell University, a recycling advocate, says that leaves "25 billion bottles" in landfills, incinerated or littered away, Business Insider says.

Pepsi has a bottled water product too – Aquafina. Don't just glance over the brand name. The name is meant to give you the feeling that this is "fine water." The bottle is filled with tap water. Pretty fine.

Both Dasani and Aquafina take much of their water from California, which is suffering from a record-breaking drought (source:http://www.motherjones.com/environment/2014/08/bottled-water-california-drought).

How this is even possible is something somebody is going to have to ask California government officials.

This is the reality of the bottled water industry. But consumers don't want to know the facts. They have purchased a dream. The dream they are buying is helping to destroy the environment. This is an unpleasant fact that most bottled water consumers probably don't want to hear about.

Besides Pepsi and Aquafina, PepsiCo owns a number of snack food brands, including Fritos, Tostitos, Cheetos, Doritos and Lay's. It's the leading snack food company in the world (source: Rainforest Action Network).

Doritos' is for "For the Bold," as their 2016 Super Bowl commercial says. Doritos portrays the chips as fun and just a little crazy to appeal to the young boys it wants to sell to. You'll see guys playing sports and staring at well-built women on the beach, or in the park. Also, you'll see constant munching of Doritos with the distinctive crunch.

For the new Doritos Mix product, made of four shapes with nacho cheese, spicy nacho, jumpin' jack cheese and, four cheese (which provides a Cheese Explosion, didn't you know?) the first commercial showed a beautiful young female newscaster eating a Mix chip, looking aroused with excitement, then jumping and down in the TV studio on a pogo stick. Subtle, it's not. The commercial also shows various men and women around the world eating the snack and jumping around and dancing in the streets. One person shoots out of a cannon.

Sorry to try to stop the guy from blowing out of the cannon, but PepsiCo, major provider of major fun, is a big contributor to destroying rainforests in Indonesia. Companies are razing the rainforest there to make palm oil plantations. Palm oil is an important ingredient in PepsiCo's products. They're tearing down an enormous rainforest for snack food.

And a lot of other products as well, from lipstick, soap and shampoo to pizza dough, bread, cookies, chocolate and ice cream.

As the World Wildlife Fund puts it, "You might not cook with it, but you almost certainly eat or use palm oil. Palm oil is the most widely consumed vegetable oil on the planet, and it is in about half of all packaged products sold in the supermarket. While palm oil is the most efficient source of vegetable oil, its rapid expansion threatens some of the planet's most important and sensitive habitats. Palm oil grows in tropical rainforests, and the uncontrolled clearing of these forests for conventional palm oil plantations has led to widespread loss of these irreplaceable and biodiverse rich forests. Plantations have also been connected to the destruction of habitat of endangered species, including orangutans, tigers, elephants and rhinos."

Sum of Us, an organization devoted to developing a sustainable global economy, describes on its web site the consequences of what Pepsi and other snack food companies are doing for palm oil:

"Deforestation in Southeast Asia has made Indonesia the third largest carbon emitter on Earth...the remaining forests of Indonesia are storing as much carbon dioxide as the entire Earth emits in a year, meaning that allowing the destruction to continue could detonate a carbon bomb."

PepsiCo isn't the only company involved. Also helping to obliterate the Indonesian rainforest are the following companies, many well-known to the American consumer: Campbell Soup, ConAgra, Dunkin' Donuts, General Mills, Grupo Bimbo, Hillshire Brands, Heinz, Hormel Foods, Kellogg Company, Kraft Food, Krispy Kreme, Mars, Mondelez, Nestle, Nissin Foods, Hershey, J.M. Smucker,

Toyo Suisan Kaisha, and Unilever (source: Rainforest Action Network, or RAN). All these companies make "a wide range of popular snack foods in the United States and abroad" that contain palm oil from the Indonesian rain forest.

Mondelez, based in Deerfield, Illinois, owns so many popular and historical American brands that I was nearly blinded by the number of product logos displayed on the company's web site, including Oreos, Fig Newton's, Chips Ahoy! Nutter Butter, Nilla Wafers, Philadelphia Cream Cheese, Honey Maid Graham Crackers, Cadbury, Triscuit, Wheat Thins, Trident, Dentyne and many other products. They operate in 165 countries and have net revenues of approximately $30 billion yearly.

Another corporate behemoth is Red Bull, which basically created the energy drink market. Red Bull is not destroying the rainforest, but it is a major consumer of aluminum for its cans.

Red Bull is the leader in the market –operating in 169 countries and with a 70 to 90 percent market share in 100 of those countries– Boom! (source: Selling Power magazine), offers its consumers wild, energy-charged dreams, reflecting the values of the drink, which is supposed to give you super extra energy and alertness. It has 80 milligrams of caffeine, taurine, which is an amino acid, and 27 grams of sugars in one 8.46 ounce can.

Red Bull is now stitched into global youth culture. The company sponsors more than 500 extreme sport athletes. Its web site and numerous TV channels offer videos, news articles and photos of wind surfers challenging monster waves, cliff diving, mountain biking on "terrifying trails" (quoting from their web site) down Arizona rock mountain cliffs and switchbacks, rally cross --- car racing on dirt or grass, motorbike racing, ocean racing – anything that involves adrenaline-fueled, thrill-seeking, death-defying sports, as well as something called e-sports, which is actually video gaming for those Red Bull fans who want to get their competitive, macho thrills from the seat of their pants.

An extreme, or "free" skier on the international Red Bull extreme skiing team, was killed in an avalanche in Chile on July 18th, 2016. Matilda Rapaport had survived one avalanche before, but even after surviving that close call, she skied on peaks she could reach only by helicopter. She was 30 years old and had been married three months, to her high school sweetheart (source: New York Times, 7/29/2016).

Red Bull "herds consumers to exclusive and exciting events that get high media coverage. Red Bull supports close to 500 world-class extreme sports athletes that compete in spectacular and often record-breaking events across the globe," Dietrich Mateschitz, the company's founder, told

Selling Power magazine. "We don't bring the product to the consumer, we bring consumers to the product."

Herd is a good word for what they do. It implies that consumers are little more than cattle. Red Bull has built the fences of this particular global ranch and created the herd to storm into the places where the company can zap the willing millions into reaching for Red Bull's energy drinks.

Red Bull has its own record label for rap, hip-hop and disco music. Its sponsors concerts and music festivals and offers aspiring musicians regularly scheduled academies with lectures, workshops and recording sessions, all over the world, from Istanbul to Montreal. The New York Red Bulls are a team in Major League Soccer in the U.S. Of course, they play in Harrison, New Jersey, which makes you wonder how they can be called a New York team. But never mind the reality – they're selling you a line that they're from New York.

The point of all these activities is to sell the dream of living life on the edge, the very edge of life and death, where anything is possible, where the incredible rush of adrenaline hits you right in the middle of your chest, all yours, if you drink Red Bull!

The truth in my neighborhood is that I see a couple of discarded cans of Red Bull just about every day, lying in the gutter or on the sidewalk, probably bought by teenagers from the local high school. Are the buyers sky diving, or running up mountains or surfing giant waves? No, but they're living the dream of Red Bull – the daring, adventure-crazed heroes, who passionately live in the moment, who revel in extreme recklessness, who live on the edge. The edge of what is the question. The edge of sanity maybe, because it's all a grand illusion sold to you in order to sell you more Red Bull.

The illusion sells incredibly well – six billion cans in 2015 (source: statista.com).

Now let's talk about reality. Of course, Red Bull provides society with the same issues of litter and landfilling their cans as any other can maker.

Red Bull's cans are recyclable. But do Red Bull users seem like the kind of people who will recycle an aluminum can?

No way! These guys are way too tough! They are too busy surfing 100-foot-high waves, diving off cliffs or climbing the outside of the Empire State Building with a grand piano tied to their leg to bother with recycling.

They drink the can, then drop it in the dirt. That's where I found an orphaned can with my daughter, outside my apartment building on July 5, 2016 at 6:32 pm. The tough Red Bull guy who drank it and threw it on the ground was nowhere in sight.

Maybe Red Bull can use some of its considerable resources to educate its users on why they need to recycle. Unless Red Bull can somehow make recycling seem cool, the users will never do it.

Aside from that depressing fact, Red Bull is a drug. It will make your heart rate and blood pressure rise within minutes after drinking it (source: http://www.dailymail.co.uk/femail/food/article-3196220/What-happens-body-24-hours-drink-Red-Bull.html).

For the next 40 to 50 minutes, you are supposed to feel increasingly alert and able to concentrate better. In an hour, the body may suffer a sugar crash. The caffeine may also start wearing off. After the drug fully wears off, about 12 to 24 hours later, the user may well become irritable and suffer headaches and constipation (Question: Should Red Bull sponsor a toilet bowl competition?). The effects diminish with continued usage, so you need to drink more Red Bull to get the same effect on your body.

Other energy drink makers taking on Red Bull have stuffed their cans with even more caffeine. Monster, the number two global seller (source: caffeineinformer.com) sells a 16 ounce can with 160 milligrams of caffeine. Red Bull's can is a little more than eight ounces, with 80 grams. So, Monster has the same amount of caffeine, but double the dose. Because who is going to buy a 16 ounce can and not drink all of it? (Red Bull also has a 16 ounce can, but it only has 77 mg of caffeine.)

Also, Monster offers larger doses in its cans – up to 188 mg. The name and logo of Monster is meant to appeal to those on-the-edge teens. What teenage boy doesn't want to be a monster, with the jagged green claws you see on that black can? Being a monster means being powerful and kind of crazy. Good for scaring people!

Among the various extreme sports Monster underwrites is bull riding. One of their sponsored athletes is named Chase Outlaw, a very rodeo tough kid from Arkansas. How's that for branding?

His parents are actually named Outlaw and they actually named their son Chase. Is Chase an outlaw or will he chase one for you? His favorite hat is "American" and his favorite food is "fast," says the championship bull riding website. He's a good representative for Monster, no question.

Monster also sponsors ultimate fighting, which is basically a contest where two incredibly well-muscled men and women try to beat the living crap out of each other, using fists, feet, elbows, knees. It's boxing, wresting, mixed martial arts-- a vicious mix. I saw a match on You Tube. Half of the loser's face was smashed with his blood, as was the mat where the men scrapped, in a fight that lasted less than five minutes.

Monster has its own cheerleading squads of sexed-up girls in small tops to reveal lots of breast flesh, wearing the Monster logo on their little shorts (cinched with a white belt). About 65 million people around the world are fans of ultimate fighting (source: cagepotato.com).

Monster also sponsors Kurt Busch, a leading NASCAR driver who has won 28 races (source: Wikipedia). In early 2015 Busch was suspended from the NASCAR tour for allegedly choking and beating up his girlfriend. He reportedly smashed her head against a wall in Busch's motor home (source: espn.go.com). However, no charges were ever proven. Busch is on the racetrack and Monster is one of his proud sponsors.

Then there's the 5-Hour Energy Drink, which has 200 mg of caffeine in a two-ounce bottle. Sales of the company's extra-strength cherry flavor is "benefiting" the Special Operations Warrior Foundation ("Help support the families of our fallen heroes," its website says), by devoting an unspecified amount of profits from this product's sale to the foundation. However noble it might be, this sponsorship is fully consistent with the company's marketing of its product as a living-on-the-edge offering for heroes and over-achievers.

My first and only hands-on experience with the 5-Hour Energy Drink product was finding the little plastic bottles on the sidewalks and gutters and garbage cans of my town, discarded by teens. Then I started noticing them on the front counter of the local stationary store, which actually seems to make most of its money selling lottery tickets. The store is just about the worst place in the world to convey the 5-Hour Energy brand, but in actuality it conveys the tawdriness of the product quite well, an unintended message.

Can 5-Hour Energy drink hurt you? Since I have never ingested the product myself, I went to the web. Injuryrisks.com says that it can cause something called niacin flush, a burning sensation on your face and legs and turn your skin temporarily red. 5-Hour Energy is overloaded with niacin, because, the manufacturer says, niacin converts proteins, fats, carbohydrates and starches into energy. Niacin flush isn't dangerous, but uncomfortable and maybe not the best thing to drink before you go out on a date.

Worse, 5-Hour Energy can cause dizziness, nausea and vomiting. It can give you heart palpitations (a rapid, fluttering or pounding heartbeat), insomnia, chest pain and numbness in your arms and legs. You're living on the edge when you drink 5-Hour Energy, right? So, what if you can't sleep or get chest pain? Who cares? You're a big, brave teenage consumer, fighting to live life to its fullest.

Starbucks presents a far different problem. Its mission statement says, "Inspiring and nurturing the human spirit – one person, one cup and one neighborhood at a time."

This is ambitious stuff. Starbucks has created a culture of hanging out, all by itself. The stores are far more mellow and appealing than your usual fast food shop, such as the omnipresent McDonald's. The stores send out this message to me -- Enjoy the rich coffee, do some work on your laptop, stay awhile. Relax. Let's get mellow. With more than 22,000 stores in about 70 countries, Starbucks gives consumers lots of coffeehouses to satisfy their cravings for coffee, tea, exotic baked goods and mood music.

Starbucks has a Facebook video of a barista in Seattle, Daniel, who makes a cup of coffee in the back of his vehicle, then goes hiking in the mountains. The video features Daniel tramping through the woods, over streams and rocks. Tall green trees decorate the landscape and Daniel enjoys being here, alone with the quiet serenity of nature, his thoughts, and his Starbucks coffee.

Starbucks' web site says the company has hired more than 6,000 military veterans, with the goal of hiring almost 4,000 more. It wants to help alleviate youth unemployment, assist paying college costs for its employees, and help coffee farmers, among many other projects. It says it cares about recycling and climate change. The company is trying to lower its carbon footprint. This is self-preservation, as the company acknowledges that the world needs a stable climate in order for coffee trees to grow.

However!

Starbucks' own website states:

"Our customers' ability to recycle our cups…is dependent upon multiple factors, including local government policies and access to recycling markets such as paper mills and plastic processors…Some communities readily recycle our paper and plastic cups, but with operations in 70 countries, Starbucks faces a patchwork of recycling infrastructure and market conditions. Additionally, in many of our stores landlords control the waste collection and decide whether or not they want to provide recycling. These challenges require recycling programs be customized to each store and market and may limit our ability to offer recycling in some stores."

Starbucks enjoyed $2 billion in net income in 2015, on sales of $19 billion. I think these guys can try to do a better job of getting a handle on paper and plastic recycling, instead of hemming and hawing like this on their web site. They could theoretically create a recycling education program for high school kids, as well as local governments and landlords (yes!). They can tell the landlords, we are making money for you, so maybe you can help us out a little too, on this very important environmental issue.

As far as climate change, Starbucks tells us about more problems than it is solving. Again to its web site: "Given that our agronomists, quality experts and buyers are on the ground working with coffee farmers every day, we see firsthand and hear directly about the impacts of climate change. In addition to increased erosion and infestation by pests and coffee rust, coffee farmers are reporting shifts in rainfall and harvest patterns that are hurting their communities and shrinking the available usable land in coffee regions around the world.

"The potential impact of climate change on farming communities is a key reason addressing our environmental impact is a priority for Starbucks. We believe now is the time to increase our investments in solutions and strategies – both in our stores and at the farm level – that help tackle this crisis."

To its credit, Starbucks is doing lots of things to try to fight climate change. The corporation purchases renewable energy, builds stores that are energy and water-efficient advocates for "stronger climate change and clean energy policies," through the Business for Innovative Climate and Energy Policy group.

Despite all this positive activity, Starbucks' greenhouse gas emissions are increasing. Again, to their credit, this information is on their web site. The site says that in 2011 the company generated more than 1.1 million metric tons of carbon dioxide. In 2015, the company had increased its emissions to 1,342,419 metric tons.

How did this happen?

Starbucks says: "Emissions increased 6.7 percent through net store growth, and because some of our energy savings have been offset by the growth of our business into new sectors that have altered our environmental footprint in unanticipated ways. For example, the addition of heated food to our menu has required an increase in refrigeration and ovens, offsetting a portion of the gains from our existing energy efficiency measures."

I appreciate the company's honesty, but most consumers are not going to be a nerd like me and dive into the corporate responsibility section to find out all this information for themselves. Starbucks has good intentions, but they're still mucking things up in terms of carbon emissions. I'm sure they would have generated more carbon emissions if the company had not implemented its clean energy and green building programs. But whatever they've done is not enough.

Now, for the king of "I'm Lovin' It" – McDonald's.

It has 36,000 stores in more than 100 countries. McDonald's is more similar to Starbucks than you might think. For one, it has a very distinctive brand – it is the ultimate family friendly restaurant. What Disney is to kids' entertainment, McDonald's is to kids' food. Also, like Starbucks, McDonald's is a big champion of environmental responsibility, but it's falling short.

One recent commercial features a kid who just won't smile for her school picture. She won't smile, period, until Daddy picks her up in the family's SUV. On the back seat is a happy meal. The kid smiles as widely as possible, and shouts out, "Thanks, Dad!" I love this kid. She's so happy!

I grew up with the golden arches. I remember when I was about seven years old my grandfather took my three brothers and me to dinner at a McDonald's sitting on a major road, about 1965. I loved McDonald's. The crispy fries, the hamburgers, the buns, the soda.

My daughter loved the place for a long time too. She liked to order chicken sandwiches, then run around in the playground, with long tubes and tunnels. She loved to get Happy Meals, which offer a little plastic toy with it. Millions of people have warm memories of McDonald's.

Kids can get Angry Birds toys, Secret Lives of Pets toys, Power Puff girl toys and Skylanders Super Chargers vehicle toys (from a video game). McDonald's is just good, clean fun, right?

I tried to find out if McDonald's has any kind of estimate on the quantity of greenhouse gases its operations emit. The web site doesn't feature anything like Starbucks data. That's a big black hole of information I would like to dig into.

McDonald's is trying to eliminate deforestation in their products, as well as reduce their carbon pollution, according to their website. They have made some important pledges:

"We will focus our initial efforts on beef, fiber-based packaging, palm oil, coffee, and soy used for beef & poultry feed, given their link to deforestation."

Also: "Beef: McDonald's supports the sustainable production of beef...We are developing goals and will begin purchasing a portion of our beef from verified, sustainable sources starting in 2016.

"Palm Oil: By 2020, our goal is for 100% of the palm oil used in our restaurants worldwide and as an ingredient in McDonald's products to be verified as having come from a system that supports sustainable palm oil production. We will continue encouraging McDonald's palm oil suppliers to move toward traceable and transparent palm oil supply chains as a way to ensure no deforestation.

"Fiber: By 2020, our goal is to source 100% of fiber-based packaging from recycled or certified sources. As the first global restaurant business in World Wildlife Fund's (WWF) Global Forest & Trade Network, we support its initiative to eliminate illegal logging and transform the global marketplace to save the world's valuable and threatened forests.

"Coffee: By 2020, our goal is to have 100% of our coffee verified as supporting sustainable production. We will work with globally recognized programs and provide support for coffee farmers through initiatives such as our technical assistance project in Guatemala."

I hope McDonald's can do all this. If they do, I'll be glad. However, there is a big hole in their planning. Number one, their milk bottles are made of plastic, which comes from oil. And, those Happy Meal toys need a lot of oil and plastic to make. The Joker and Batman toys I bought for my daughter in suburban Maryland in 2015 have imprinted on them, "Made for McDonald's 2015 China CBT China." On her toy shelf, I found a Frankenstein from "Hotel Transylvania," made in Vietnam.

Like its overall carbon emissions, McDonald's Happy Meal toy production is a big question. With its toys made in China and Vietnam, which offer cheap and environmentally questionable production, McDonald's has a lot of carbon dioxide emissions on its hands which can't be quantified, which is convenient for them. An email I sent to the McDonald's press office asking about the company's carbon emissions went unanswered (McDonald's requests that all media inquiries be done by email, not phone call.).

That kid in the Happy Meal commercial, the one who smiled when she saw the box with the Golden Arches? Her smile comes with a price -- the price of carbon pollution to make the toy and food and packaging in the box.

In fact, there are of course an enormous number of stores and companies that have outsourced production to China, which is the biggest carbon emitter in the world (source: Wikipedia). It is wrong to pin all this carbon pollution on China. Yes, China needs to work much harder to clean up their factories and drastically cut the scandalous amounts of carbon dioxide they are generating daily. But American corporations are part of this enormous problem too. American companies such as Wal-Mart and Apple are famous for outsourcing production to China. Everyone wants a cheap price, right? The result is that America and China are, in a very real sense, co-dependent economies, and the U.S. should share a good portion of the responsibility for all the carbon China is emitting.

Advertising -- Moving

Dodge Ram – those two no-nonsense names tell you "Big Strong Man, With Big Strong Truck!" One recent commercial shows men cutting down extremely large trees, then hauling them away in the clean mountain air, using a Dodge Ram truck. Sam Elliott, whose voice can cut through razor wire, narrates.

It's bad enough they have to pollute the air with this monster, but they do they have to kill the trees too? We might need those trees! You know, to fight global warming. The global warming you are helping to accelerate by buying and using that big, bad truck.

The Dodge Ram commercials feature this little triangle at the end – Guts-Glory-Ram."

In another commercial, young men are seen diving off cliffs, riding motorbikes and driving their Dodge Ram trucks on dirt plains with mountains in the background. Sam Elliott, his voice full of gravity, says, "This is the life of a rebel."

Um, no it isn't. This is the life of a thrill-seeking adventurer who wants an adrenaline rush. A rebel is someone who actually challenges the established order. All these guys are doing are buying big trucks which spew carbon pollution out their thick, solid tailpipes. More testosterone, anyone?

Matching up against it is the Ford F-150, which hard-bitten narrator Denis Leary declares is "the future of tough."

A few regular guys (not actors), featured in a Chevy Silverado commercial, called the 2016 Silverado "aggressive" and "bad ass." Another commercial shows small front end loader dumping stone blocks into the truck beds of the Silverado and a Ford F-150, to find out which truck bed is tougher.

The Honda Ridgeline has a rock drop commercial on YouTube as well. GMC Trucks has a model called the Sierra Denali. By themselves Sierra and Denali exude macho — you've got the Sierra from the Sierra Nevada mountain range, which consists mostly of granite, and Denali, the biggest mountain in North America, out in Alaska — the toughest frontier in the U.S. Denali means "The Tall One." Put Sierra and Denali together and you have a double macho truck. There's also a Yukon Denali. What can top that? The Mojave Everest? Death Valley Alps?

Toyota has the Tundra and the Tacoma — rough and tough names, alright. Nissan has the Titan and the Frontier.

Real men drive real trucks. But do real men make real pollution?

Then there's Jeep. You have the Jeep Renegade (there's that rebel thing again), Cherokee, Grand Cherokee, Wrangler, the Wrangler Unlimited, and the Patriot. Mitsubishi has the Lancer and the Outlander. Subaru has the Forester and the Outback. Nissan has the Rogue.

I'll stop now. You get the idea.

Motor vehicle commercials are one of the purest examples of consumer culture ever invented. You travel alone, a rugged man (or woman) riding in a landscape where there are no other people. You can escape it all.

Consumer culture has trained vehicle buyers to get the biggest, most heavily armored truck to satisfy their immediate needs for a dream that isn't real. Caring about the environmental damage these beasts spew every day isn't part of the message, and therefore, not valued.

For proof, when gas prices go down, truck sales go up. Truck buyers are simply responding to the price mechanism. They want as big a vehicle as possible, as cheaply as possible. If gas prices go up, truck sales go down. This presents a great argument for raising gasoline taxes to levels seen in Germany, but of course, in America, any proposal to raise gas taxes is met with vehement protests.

S.U.V. commercials are similar to the trucks. Mercedes emphasizes that its vehicles and its drivers outperform everyone else, because they have more guts. A recent Land Rover commercial narrator explains: "Adventure – it's in our DNA." Ford says its SUVs are "unstoppable." Their 2016 commercial announces, "Life is a sport. We are the utility."

Speaking of which, is there a product more misnamed than Sport Utility Vehicle? There is no sport involved in driving SUVs on the road, unless you weigh their tonnage against an ordinary car. How many people take their SUVs off-road, or up mountain paths? Most people on the road use them for transporting their kids. The SUV title offers people the opportunity to dream of what they could do with the vehicle, versus what they actually do with it every day – drive to work, pick up the kids from school, go out to a restaurant.

Contrary to the picture of the open road (or off-road) in the commercials, our highways are jammed with trucks, SUVs and cars all choking on each other's exhaust pipes. There is no romance here.

During every evening rush, I sit in traffic with my little Honda Civic, surrounded by SUVs and trucks at least twice the size of my car. In a way, I can see the results of an evolutionary arms race among motor vehicles. Cars have grown into SUVs and consumer trucks. The bigger they are, the more intimidating and threatening they can be to other motorists. So, the commercials are also appealing to potential buyers because of the size of the SUV or truck.

The traffic snakes along at five, maybe ten miles an hour. People constantly honk at each other, curse, cut each other off and act in a generally nasty way. Where is the open road, with its clean, pure air? Where can I be alone? Is it possible that people are frustrated in part because the dream they bought isn't delivering?

Here the drivers are mobbed by thousands of other people in their own "shiny metal boxes," as pop singer Sting would say, and it's frustrating as hell. Where did the dream from the commercial go? How come we don't have that? Was it all a lie? To ask the question is to answer it.

It can take me up to an hour to drive 10 miles from my job to my apartment building. In the morning, I leave early (six AM) and the same drive takes about 25 minutes.

You can easily see the same phenomenon, but in much worse form, in Los Angeles, San Francisco, Seattle, Boston, Philadelphia, Houston, Dallas and Chicago. Again, reality defeats the manufacturers' illusions of freedom and power.

The transportation sector causes more than one-quarter of all the greenhouse gas emissions in the country, according to the U.S. Federal Highway Administration (FHA).

"Last year, Americans drove almost three trillion miles according to estimates from the FHA," states the tree-planting non-profit group American Forests. "That's a lot of time on the open road, time stuck in traffic jams, and time for carbon emissions to enter our atmosphere."

How much carbon pollution do our cars put into the air? American Forests says: "…more than four tons of new greenhouse gas are floating around our atmosphere each year for every car on the road!"

"More people die in Southern California from air pollution related diseases than from traffic accidents and crime-related incidents combined," states Earthjustice, an environmental legal organization in its Summer 2016 newsletter.

Motorcycle commercials offer a fairly close parallel to trucks and SUVs in terms of their messages. A recent Harley-Davidson commercial asks – "What do we get from running with a different crowd? Inspiration." The end of the commercial shows various bikers gathered around some old wood pallets in a clearing in the forest, which one of the men lights on fire.

The Indian Motorcycle company "forged its legend with steel and grit…Every Scout is its own legend. It's time to start yours," implying that riding this cycle will help you experience the adventures you crave.

BMW Motorrad demands, "Make Life a Ride."

The 2014 BMW commercial is similar to Red Bull's approach – embrace thrills and have fun. The commercial says, "It's time to be impatient...don't settle...ride...find your own path...wherever you're going, it won't be boring."

A 2016 commercial for the BMW S1000RR commands that this motorbike is "Your Mission to Ride." The commercial has no narration – just the sights and sounds of a BMW zipping around a steel-gray warehouse that seems to want to entrap the rider. He escapes just as the door to the place is closing.

A late 2015 home-made video posted on YouTube about this model, prompted this comment: "The 2016 BMW S1000R is the same as the 2015...100 percent badass, rip your head off, legal insanity..."

There is the dream laid out – the inspirations, the legends, the mission to ride. Let's talk about the reality. The costs of riding these machine are considerable, to both the rider and everybody else.

"Motorcyclists are overrepresented in crashes and fatalities," states the Governors Highway Safety Association" on its website. "In 2014, 4,486 motorcyclists lost their lives on America's roads."

The Insurance Information Institute's June, 2016 report says that more than eight million motorcycles on the road in 2014, "92,000 motorcyclists were injured, up 4.5 percent from 88,000 in 2013. In 2013, motorcyclists were about 26 times more likely than passenger car occupants to die in a crash per vehicle mile traveled and five times more likely to be injured."

That's a lot of risk for a thrill ride, not just for the rider, but to other motorists and citizens. The Insurance Information Institute quoted the U.S. Government Accounting Office (GAO) as estimating that in 2010 "motorcycle crashes cost $16 billion in direct costs such as emergency services, medical costs, including rehabilitation, property damage, loss of market productivity including lost wages, loss in household productivity and insurance costs, including claims and the cost of defense attorneys."

In its report the GAO recommended that the National Highway Transportations Safety Agency (NHTSA) increase the amount of money it spends on state programs to improve motorcycle safety. The NHTSA spent almost $46 million for this purpose from 2006 to 2012. That's taxpayer money. We all pay for the thrill ride the motorcycle companies are selling to those who want to live on the extreme edge.

Off-road vehicles, or all-terrain vehicles (ATVs) present related issues. A Yamaha commercial for its ATVs shows a rider tearing up forested trails, mountain ridges and sand dunes. These vehicles grind through mud, spike up hills and burn by lakes and ponds. These things are just wild, crazy fun, especially for kids who don't yet have a driver's license.

I call this approach, "Let me enjoy nature while I destroy it at the same time."

While you need to be at least 16 years of age to drive a car, this is not the case with an ATV.

The Federal government does not regulate ATVs. This is the province of the states. In many states, from Kentucky and Iowa to North Dakota and Connecticut, a 12-year old child can ride an ATV. In North Carolina and Pennsylvania, an eight-year old can. In Texas and New Mexico, you can be six years old and ride on an ATV (source: National Conference of State Legislatures, 1/1/2014).

You might think to yourself, "Can't the kids get hurt?"

They can and they do. More than 13,000 people have been killed on ATVs from 1982 to 2014 (source: Consumer Product Safety Commission/CPSC). About 3,000 of these fatalities were of children younger than 16.

In 2014, 385 people were reported killed using ATVs. In that same year, "there were an estimated 93,700 ATV-related, emergency department-treated injuries in the United States. An estimated 26 percent of these involved children younger than 16 years of age," the CPSC says on its web site. "The 2014 estimated ATV-related, emergency-department treated injuries primarily affected the following body parts: head or neck, arm (the shoulder down), leg, and the torso."

Additionally, besides the hospital and insurance costs that are often passed onto the public, we all pay in additional, important way. These vehicles are allowed to speed through our national forests and a number of state parks, and their effects are not benign.

New Hampshire, Missouri and South Carolina allow ATV riding in their state parks, for example. So do Texas, Oklahoma and Louisiana.

"The noise and pollution from dirt bikes, ATVs and other off-road vehicles adversely affect America's national forests and the plants, animals and humans that depend on these great places," explains the Wilderness Society's (WS) web site.

"The majority of national forest visitors hike, bike, camp or fish, for example. For these visitors, off-road vehicles can be a source of pollution and loud noise in the very place we go to get away from it all," the WS web site says. "Although only 1.5 percent of people use off-road vehicles, this small minority can have an out-sized impact on others if not properly managed. Off-road vehicles can also have devastating consequences for the plants, animals and ecosystems that make up our national forests.

"For example, wildlife, such as elk and bobcats, avoid areas used by off-road vehicles. This creates boundaries that can cut off food supplies and other necessities." Also, the WS web says, "off-road vehicles spread invasive, non-native plants deep into a forest. Seeds from these non-native noxious plants are caught in the knobby tires (of the ATVs) and scattered in areas where they are incompatible with the native plants. Off-road vehicles also pollute our water...Erosion caused by fording rivers and streams has negative impacts on our national forests." Roughly one-fifth of the U.S. population depends on forests to deliver clean drinking water."

Here is another situation where consumer culture has created a product designed to excite users to seek a temporary thrill for speed, and which completely ignores the common needs of just about anyone else. Once you're fed and clothed and housed, what else is there to do? Go fast and have fun. You got a problem with that?

I do -- The ATV pollutes, it destroys habitat and it harms the water supply.

Snowmobiles and jet skis degrade the environment in similar fashion.

Wild Earth Guardians, a habitat preservation group in the western U.S., states that "off-road vehicles (ORVs) cause an extraordinary amount of habitat degradation and pollution, often in the most fragile of habitats...off-road vehicles – dirt bikes, ATVs...dune buggies, snowmobiles, jet skis, rock crawlers" (it looks like a dune buggy with giant tires) "and new multi-purpose vehicles are one of the major threats to our wildlands."

The group says on its web site that these vehicles put engine chemicals and fuels into the ground and air. They help erode streams and damage the landscape with "a web of illegal motorized paths and roads."

These vehicles can harm tundra, alpine meadows and wetlands. Plus, their loud engines disturb the people visiting these areas on foot, who are trying to experience nature the way it's meant to be experienced – in quiet. As well, I can't believe the animals who live there like the noise much.

A letter writer to Field and Stream magazine in 2008 characterized off-road vehicle users as:

"ANYONE who gets out into the backcountry has seen for themselves the massive damage done by ATVs. Not all ATV owners are irresponsible, but with great accuracy you can safely lump over 90 percent of them as over-weight gear heads who do not care about ripping up a meadow, running through spawning beds, leaving beer cans and cigarette butts and scarring up the terrain."

Field and Stream is a hunting and fishing magazine and this letter writer sounds like a fisherman. The damage off-road vehicles are wreaking is extremely alarming. Clearly, our Field and Stream writer loves woodlands. And they are being degraded by speed freaks.

Guns – Consuming a Culture of Death

The National Rifle Association (NRA) is not merely a lobbying organization threatening Federal and state lawmakers with ejection from office if they don't follow its line of keeping guns from being regulated. It's a marketing organization dedicated to spreading the gospel of buying more guns to protect yourself.

Like most other consumer messages, this is a big lie. And it's a lie that kills, every day. The NRA promises the buyer safety. What it actually delivers is death.

Gun manufacturers have donated at least $19 million to the NRA from 2005 to 2013 (source: Violence Policy Center). One of them is Remington, which makes the assault rifle that killed 20 little children and six school staff people in Sandy Hook, Connecticut on December 14, 2012.

Smith & Wesson, Beretta USA, Springfield Armory and Sturm, Ruger & Co. are all big donors to the NRA. Midway USA and Brownells also give the group money. Midway sells at least 10 different categories of bullets (source: Midway USA web site). Brownells sells replacement and upgrade parts for the AR-15, including triggers, barrels, magazines, grips and gun mounted lights, so you can see your target better in the dark (source: brownells.com). The

AR-15 was the gun used by Micah Johnson to kill five police officers in Dallas in July 2016 (source: abcnewsgo.com). The officers killed were Brent Thompson, Patrick Zamarripa, Michael Krol, Michael Smith and Lorne Ahrens.

Gavin Long used an assault rifle to kill three police officers in Baton Rouge a week later (source: WWLTV.com). The officers killed were Brad Garafola, Montrell Jackson and Matthew Gerald.

What is the vision the gun manufacturers sell to the public?

Daniel Defense tells consumers the company is "Defending Your Nation, Defending Your Home." The company sells assault rifles and pistols. I watched a video of a man using a Daniel Defense rifle on a shooting range. He pulled the trigger and bullets flew out like rockets. The video reviewer of the rifle calls it "an end of the world rifle...but it honestly just wants to shoot." (source: YouTube: AR 15 shooting review: DDM4 V1 from Daniel Defense.)

Also on YouTube, Beretta advertises its M9 pistol as made in the USA, coupled with an image of our country's flag waving in the sun, so you get the whole patriotic message right in one image. The Beretta video says the gun has "served with our troops in more than 36 countries. From the mountains of Afghanistan to the deserts of Iraq...Accuracy: 10 rounds into 3 inches at 50 yards...Proven: 600,00 pistols delivered to the U.S. DOD (Department of Defense) ... 30 years as the official sidearm of the U.S. Military...America's #1 Pistol...The M9 – reliable, accurate, proven."

The video shows two men wearing military gear methodically searching a house, then shooting in the desert against the setting sun, with ominous music in the background to signal danger.

The message comes down to this: The manufacturers want prospective buyers to identify with the military aspect of the weapon. Soldiers protect the country. You can protect your country and your home by using this gun. This gun will help you keep you and your family safe. Men get the message that they are performing in their rightful roles as protectors and defenders.

As Ice-T puts it "the right to bear arms is because that's the last form of defense against tyranny" (source: Chuck Woolery video on YouTube).

Chuck Woolery is a gun rights activist, Christian minister and former game show host (Wheel of Fortune, 1975-1981 and Love Connection – source: Wikipedia). Chuck Woolery says in the video that one of the reasons we need guns is to prevent an invasion of the country by a foreign power.

If China and Russia wanted to attack us, I have a pretty good feeling they wouldn't be invading. If they invaded, these guys would be using their navies and air forces. Our military would see them coming by sea or air pretty fast, and they would defend us with all kinds of cruise missiles, aircraft carriers, submarines, you name it. Our country has the world's biggest military and we'll use it if we need to. What are men with handguns and assault rifles going to do? Stand on Laguna Beach or the Hamptons waiting for the invaders to land at the coasts in order to defend the country?

So that leaves nukes. If China wanted to nuke us, no number of guns in all the world will defend our country against that. We'll nuke them. But we'll all be dead and the world will be destroyed, so this is kind of self-defeating for China, which seems to manufacture just about anything Americans buy.

The Russians are another matter. Putin seems pretty dangerous. He took over Crimea. He's bombing Syria. If Putin wanted to nuke us, we'd get the same result. Most of America will be devastated and we'll nuke them. The approximately 300 million guns Americans own won't do a damn thing against one nuclear-tipped missile.

Now let's look at who else might want to invade the U.S. – our closest neighbors. Mexico could, right? Well, maybe not. The United States is "Mexico's largest trading partner and largest foreign investor" (source: U.S. Department of State). I don't know about Chuck Woolery, but I'm not lying awake at night thinking the Mexican Army is going to invade the country.

That leaves, now let me think for a minute. Yes, Canada! Canada is certainly ready to invade. Let's buy more guns to defend ourselves against those vicious, barbarian hordes from Canada, who will make us play ice hockey and pour maple syrup on our pancakes against our will!

I like Chuck Woolery. He's a very funny guy. Tell that invasion joke again, Chuck.

Smith & Wesson advertises two of its handguns as ways to "shield yourself." It portrays a young, attractive white woman running through the streets of a rough looking, empty neighborhood in the city. She has a concealed gun wrapped around her waist, so she can run with no fear. It also shows a young, white man taking his concealable gun with him as he goes out for coffee. He walks by alleys, against an empty urban neighborhood where danger could be lurking at any moment. With his gun, he can get his coffee, no problem.

Implicit in this commercial is the premise that cities are dangerous places for white people. But they can protect themselves from minorities who lurk around each alleyway and abandoned house.

That's the promise to gun buyers – that they can protect themselves and their families. Now let's talk about the extremely grim reality.

When I was a boy, about seven years old, I went to a summer day camp which had pistol shooting as one of its activities.

We shot at little concentric targets. The bullets were blanks. One of the rules at the shooting range was if someone had finished shooting and was checking their target, the next person in line had to wait before shooting. Sensible rule, right?

One day I shot at my target, then went to check what I had hit. As I was looking at the paper, another boy fired a shot. It hit about two or three feet away from me.

Yes, the bullets were blanks, but I freaked out in a very loud way, complaining to the counselor that the kid's shot had almost hit me.

The one big lesson I learned right there is that it's really easy to hurt someone with a gun, even accidentally. It's extremely easy to break the rules of gun safety.

And Americans break them all the time.

Sha'quille Kornegay, two years old, of Kansas City, Missouri, found a loaded handgun under her father's pillow in April, 2016 while they were supposed to be napping in bed. She accidentally shot herself in the head and died (source: New York Times, May 5, 2016). She was buried in a little pink coffin.

Veronica Rutledge of Blackfoot, Idaho, 29 years old, was killed in a Walmart store by her two-year old son, who had grabbed her gun out of his Mom's purse, then shot her by accident (source: CNN, 12/31/2014). I wonder how that kid is going to feel growing up, knowing that he shot his own mother? What kind of adult is he going to be?

Caroline Starks, an adorable, blonde-haired, two-year old toddler from Kentucky, was accidentally shot in the chest by her five-year old brother, who used a .22 caliber rifle purchased for him as a gift. The gun was a single-shot rifle marketed to kids as "My First Rifle," by the Keystone Sporting Arms company. The mother had stepped out of the house for a few minutes and her son started playing with the gun, unsupervised (source: Daily Mail, 4/30/2013).

Then there are the people who want to use their guns to kill.

Christy Sheats killed both of her grown daughters in front of her husband, in June 2016, in Katy, Texas. The older daughter was to be married three days before she was murdered by her own Mom. Christy Sheats was reportedly suffering from anxiety and depression. The mother apparently wanted to punish the girls' father after an argument the two had (source: Huffington Post, 6/30/2016). She aimed her gun at the police who arrived on the scene and the police shot and killed her.

Jessica White, also 29 years old, was killed in a Bronx housing project in June, 2016 (source: New York Post, 6/12/2016). She was not the intended target of the shooter, New York City police said.

To cite one more recent, horrifying example, Travon Williams, nine years old, going into the fifth grade, was shot and killed in a parking lot of a liquor and grocery store in San Bernardino, California, immediately after his father had bought a bag of candy for the boy. The boy was dancing out the door because he got the candy. His father and another person nearby were also shot and killed.

"It was 30 seconds to kill three people," the store manager said (source: LA Times, 7/8/2016). The father, 26 years old, was probably the intended target. A video of the mother grieving on the LA Times web site is wrenching. She screamed out and sobbed uncontrollably, "My baby! He was in pain! I know he was so scared! I know he was so confused...And I wasn't there. And I wasn't there!"

Think about this woman before you turn on a reality show about the Kardashians or the Real Housewives or Iron Chef. Because what happened to Travon Williams was not a scripted "reality show." It was real life. And it was ugly and awful and it betrays the lies the gun industry tells us about buying guns to protect ourselves.

Sadly, it's far too easy to write about more of these cases.

More than 32,000 people are killed by guns every year (source: Forbes.com, 8/26/2015). About 11,000 are homicides. The rest are suicides.

Since 1968, more Americans have been killed in gun-related deaths (including suicide) than have been killed in all wars America has fought since the Revolution (source: Politifact, 8/27/2015). About 1.5 million people have been killed because of guns, since 1968. About 1.396 million have been killed in our wars. "That's more than 120,130 gun deaths than war deaths...nearly four typical years' worth of gun deaths," Politifact says.

In 2011, almost 1,700 African-American kids under the age of 22, were killed by guns in the U.S. (source: USA Today, 2/11/2013, citing FBI statistics).

 "The killing of young blacks is an American pandemic," the USA Today article said. "The leading cause of death for black males ages 15-19 in those years came from the barrel of a gun. Blacks in this age group were eight times more likely than whites and two-and-a-half times more like than Hispanics to be killed by gunfire," the article stated.

Unfortunately, I don't think this is going to stop any time soon. The NRA is far too powerful and has far too much leverage over lawmakers. We couldn't get any gun legislation passed after the mass killings at Virginia Tech (2007; 32 dead), in Sandy Hook (2012; 26 dead), San Bernardino (2015; 14 dead), Charleston (2015, nine killed in a Bible study class), or Orlando (2016; 49 dead). A Republican Congress has even prevented the Centers for Disease Control (CDC) from investigating the causes of gun violence (source: politico.com, 6/24/2015).

"The CDC hasn't done any such research since 1996, when the National Rifle Association accused it of trying to use science to promote gun control," said the Politico article.

What are they afraid of finding out? Wouldn't it be worth it to find out what causes gun violence so we can try to prevent it? Too many people have died. Too many more people are going to die.

The National Rifle Association name itself is a misnomer. Sales of hunting rifles are diminishing. The NRA is not an organization of sportsmen out to hunt ducks and pheasant. Sales of assault weapons and handguns are soaring (source: huffingtonpost.com, 4/18/2013). I didn't see any commercials for hunting rifles on YouTube. But there are plenty of videos for handguns and assault weapons.

Here's the ugly truth. Gun manufacturers enjoy revenue of about $13 billion every year. Gun and ammo stores get about $3 billion a year in revenue (source: Newsmax, a conservative news web site, 12/3/2015).

The gun industry wants to expand the use of guns. They don't want to limit a good thing. Background checks would hurt sales. That's why you can be on the no-fly list, but still get a gun. In great part, because of the NRA, you can carry a gun openly in 27 states, including Texas, Florida, Nevada, Arizona, Alaska, Louisiana, Mississippi, Arkansas, Wisconsin, Michigan, Pennsylvania and Ohio (source: Wall St. Journal, 8/22/2014).

When mass shootings occur, people run out and buy more guns, because they're afraid the Federal government will finally start regulating guns (source: theintercept.com, 12/3/2015). Which never happens anyway, because of the power of the NRA. Each gun sale provides more money to the NRA for lobbying, theintercept.com article stated.

What it boils down to is this: If people must die as the gun industry profits, then that's OK with the gun manufacturers and dealers. Our Senators and Representatives will say a prayer for the dead. Then they'll go back to taking the gun industry's money so they can get re-elected and do nothing all over again.

One of the basic functions of government is to keep its citizens safe. In terms of gun crime, Congress has essentially renounced its responsibilities to do this.

I want to ask the Republican members of our government, who are preventing us from legislating gun controls: Why are you in government? Why do you want to run the country? People are killing each other on the streets, every day. More than 30,000 are dead from gun violence every year. Don't you have a duty to do something about this?

Is it simply your job to just get re-elected over and over again so you can sit in your plush chairs at your committee meetings and do nothing to help prevent people from being murdered by the thousands? What about the police officers who have been killed by assault weapons? Aren't you going to do anything about that? And if not, why not?

I don't understand how people who are against abortion don't seem to have much to say about gun violence. That includes the Republicans in Congress, from Marco Rubio to Trey Gowdy. How can they be so uncharacteristically silent in the face of the horrors of gun violence?

The Jewish people have a saying – "L'Chaim!" This means "To life!" Implicit in this phrase is the knowledge that life is precious, and often fragile. Life is good. Guns represent the opposite of that. We should hold onto life and protect it.

I wish the gun manufacturers would believe that. Instead, we are faced with a powerful industry that purports to sell protection to gun buyers but instead offers nothing but violence and death.

Entertainment -- Movies

Entertainment has become advertising in another form. Entertainment can be found everywhere, but actual information is harder to find. We're being called to consume escapism and we are doing what we're told.

"Captain America – Civil War" brought in $1 billion for Disney. "Star Wars: The Force Awakens," released in 2015, made $936 million for Disney, which also owns the ABC television network, among many other holdings. "Batman vs. Superman" made about $870 million for Time Warner, which also owns HBO, CNN, Turner Broadcasting and DC Comics, where all its superhero characters were born.

"Jurassic World," yet another movie about dinosaurs coming back to life, made $650 million for NBC Universal, which owns cable channels from "E Entertainment" to the "Weather Channel," Telemundo, the Spanish language TV network, as well as the Universal Orlando resort and many other media properties. "The Avengers: Age of Ultron," made $459 million for Disney. "The Dark Knight" gave Warner Brothers $534 million. "Transformers – Revenge of the Fallen" earned $402 million for Paramount, which is owned by Viacom. Viacom owns CBS Broadcasting and a number of cable channels, from MTV and Nickelodeon to Comedy Central and the Black Entertainment Network.

Sony Pictures' Spiderman movies have grossed more than $1 billion. Its four James Bond pictures, with Daniel Craig as 007, have brought in about $800 million.

Fox sold us "Deadpool," the sarcastic superhero with lots of guns for $363 million and the eight X-Men movies, which have sold more than $1.8 billion in tickets (source: BoxOffice Mojo.com). Fox, owned by the climate-change denying Rupert Murdoch, recently purchased the National Geographic magazine, which is disturbing to say the least. Fox also owns the over-the-top crazy conservative Fox News Channel, The Wall Street Journal newspaper, the Dow Jones news service, The New York Post tabloid, Harper Collins book publishers, and numerous newspapers in England and Australia, Murdoch's birthplace. We should all worry about this. The man is a globe-girdling giant who peddles propagandistic fantasies on his television networks.

How is entertainment like advertising? Just go to McDonald's and look at the Happy Meal toys. Or try Toys R Us. Every Star Wars picture, every Batman film, every animated cartoon pitched at kids sells toys. Our kids cannot get enough of the little Transformers toys or Superman action figures.

See a pattern here?

Most movies now sell escape and nothing but. There was a time when this was not the case. Of course, there were escape movies. There always have been. But there were also more movies about serious issues, things that happened in real life. In 1968, "2001: A Space Odyssey" showed us the beauties and terrors of space and technology. "The Graduate" showed us a college grad who didn't know what to do with himself. "The Shoes of the Fisherman" told the story of a political prisoner in the Soviet Union who is freed and becomes Pope.

"The Deer Hunter" took us to the hell of Vietnam. "Dr. Strangelove" explored the nightmare of nuclear war. "The Godfather" pictures unveiled the workings of the mob and the moral choices criminals face. "One Flew Over the Cuckoo's Nest" was all about power and what happens if you challenge it, as played out by Jack Nicholson, an inmate of a mental institution and the nurse who runs the ward where he lives.

"The China Syndrome" worried about nuclear power plants. "Scarface" showed us the drug trade in Miami. "Stand by Me," was a touching story about a childhood friendship in Oregon and their hunt for a boy who had been killed by a train. "The Outsiders" portrayed boys without parents in 1950s Tulsa. "Amadeus" distinguished between Mozart's musical genius and Salieri's mediocrity.

"Schindler's List" devastated audiences with a story of trying to survive the Holocaust in World War II. "Saving Private Ryan" blew people away with a story of D-Day and the invasion of France, exploring the hellishness of war, as well as its humanity. "Dances with Wolves" brought us the beautiful story of a U.S. Army scout meeting a Native American tribe in the Dakotas, which becomes quite sad as the tribe loses its territory to the government.

Something happened to the movies in the 2000s. "The Departed," about Boston gangsters, was a hit, but most of the best-selling pictures focused on Batman, Spiderman, new and mediocre Star Wars movies and "Lord of the Rings." Also, Disney's "Pirates of the Caribbean," broke out, which was based on a ride in the Disney parks.

Then, in the 2010s, the box office was dominated by "Star Wars – The Force Awakens," "Hunger Games," "Iron Man," "Jurassic World," "The Dark Knight Rises," "Harry Potter," "The Avengers" and "Frozen." Disney made the Star Wars, Iron Man, Avengers and Frozen movies. Disney basically killed everybody else.

In comparison, this century's films that were not about superheroes or magic schools or dinosaurs with big teeth and bad manners included "Michael Clayton," which was released in 2007. The movie's hero took on a fictional agricultural chemical corporation's threats to the health of the farmers using their products. "Michael Clayton" made $49 million. "Margin Call," about mass layoffs and financial chicanery at an investment bank took in $5 million in 2011.

"Selma," a movie about Martin Luther King and the civil rights movement, from Paramount/Viacom, made about $52 million in 2014. "12 Years A Slave, released in 2013," took in about $56 million for Fox. "Lee Daniels' The Butler," about an African-American man who served as domestic help in the White House from Eisenhower to Reagan, took in $117 million in the U.S. The film was produced by the Weinstein Company, notably, an independent studio, which doesn't have the financial pressures from shareholders that the big studios face.

"The Big Short," released in 2015, about the massive housing and financial collapse in 2007-08, made by Paramount/Viacom, took in $70 million.

"An Inconvenient Truth," the best-selling movie ever made about climate change, brought in $24 million in the U.S. in 2006, and slightly more than that from foreign audiences. In other words, this movie, about the horrible damage we are doing to our atmosphere and therefore ourselves, was more popular overseas than domestically.

Civil rights, financial collapse and climate change just aren't going to pull in Captain America-like numbers. Serious movies about serious issues have been marginalized in favor of video game action, shoot 'em up fantasies, cartoons about magic powers and cardboard visions of courage.

We're being fed junk food. And we're slopping it up, then licking the plate.

Viewers want to get caught up in the fake adventures of superheroes and dinosaur-fighting he-men, as well as laser-wielding rebels fighting a fictional empire in a galaxy nowhere near Cleveland.

Disney is the champion in this arena. It now owns the Star Wars and Marvel franchises. This is perfect. Disney is the ultimate corporate escape. It sells nothing but fantasy. What are Disneyland and Disneyworld but destinations of fake towns, beyond reality? It's a glorified amusement park.

Disney's parks represent no values except the temporary diversion of its visitors.

The castle at its heart is a place no one has ever actually lived. At the footsteps of the castle lie Main Street USA. Disney's Magic Kingdom contains a glossy simulation of Main Street USA about 1905. It's deceptively beautiful and it represents a dream of a world that no longer exists. For one, all the stores are occupied and thriving. You can buy plush toys, mouse hats, hot dogs. There's a barber shop. The street is clean to the point of neurosis. You won't see any disagreements or arguments here. You're not supposed to.

The castle's height is an illusion. The castle is just 189 feet tall. But "it benefits from a technique known as forced perspective, says Orlando Discount Tickets USA, which sells vacation package for all the vacation parks in Orlando. "The second stories of all the buildings along Main Street USA are shorter than the first stories, and the third stories are even shorter than the second, and the top windows of the castle are much smaller than they appear. The resulting visual effect is that the buildings appear to be larger and taller than they really are."

So, in other words, Disney is selling you something that isn't really there.

Disney's Animal Kingdom park is home to 2,000 animals, set down in a simulation of their real habitats. It features roller coaster rides, African native dances, and a roller coaster ride through Himalayan mountain peaks.

The Typhoon Lagoon lets you surf on artificial waves and take water rides. EPCOT tries to put across the none-too-convincing illusion that you're visiting a piece of China, England, Japan, Norway, Mexico, Germany or other countries, with prettified artificial landmarks from the countries represented. Snow White, Mary Poppins, Aladdin, Mulan and other fugitives from Disney movies haunt EPCOT, ready with a smile, a pose for the cameras with your child, and an autograph for the kiddies (using an autograph book purchased in a Disney store, of course).

OK, you say, but Disney is really targeted to children. What about adults?

We'll talk about that in the next section.

Entertainment -- TV

The ultra-hot TV show, the one that people seem to talk about endlessly online is Game of Thrones, from HBO/Time Warner. Its 2016 season finale drew 8.9 million viewers (source: New York Times, 6/28/16) and has spawned fan sites over the Internet.

HBO, the channel showing Game of Thrones, describes the show like this:

"Summers span decades. Winters can last a lifetime. And the struggle for the Iron Throne continues. It stretches from the south, where heat breeds plots, lusts and intrigues, to the vast and savage eastern lands where a young queen raises an army. All the while, in the frozen north, an 800-foot wall of ice precariously protects the war-ravaged kingdom from the dark forces that lie beyond. Kings and queens, knights and renegades, liars and lords and honest men… all play the Game of Thrones."

The show has fan sites with online conversations from viewers about who is their favorite character. Web sites debate how various plots and sub-plots are going to play out. There are spoiler alerts. The Huffington Post, a politically liberal web site which I read every day, has a whole section devoted to Game of Thrones. One article is about "The Mystery of Jon Snow's Real Name May Finally Be Solved." Another is "Littlefinger Says Jon and Sansa

Have 'New Potential On Game of Thrones." One more: "Why Jaime Might Kill Cersei On Game of Thrones."

Kids didn't write these articles for other kids. These aren't comic books.

Consumer culture has allowed adults to turn themselves into children again. This show is just one example of the horror of this metamorphosis, which we have accomplished ourselves. We are killing our adulthood.

Adults are spending way too much time on raw escapism. Is this who are? A bunch of children gaping at fictional adventures where nothing real is at stake?

The 2016 season finale for the zombie show The Walking Dead scored 14 million viewers (source: TVbythenumbers.com). Zombies are everywhere on the planet, threatening the relatively few normal humans left.

The people watching this show should have their own show. Let's call it, "Nights of the Sitting Dead." In this show, we have millions of so-called living people starting transfixed at a large, flat screen filled with other people who are sickened by a pathogen and brought to a state of disgusting decay, to chase real people who are still alive.

The show even has its own after-show, The Talking Dead. I'd say, people get a life, but I'm not sure they have one.

We've also got Dancing with the Stars, The Bachelorette and America's Got Talent, more mind-numbing balm on mile-wide screens for the masses. Like Seinfeld, the shows really are about nothing. They're essentially competition shows which create and run inside a closed and cloistered world of their own, in which no outside reality can intrude.

Which brings me to Andy Cohen. The shows this man produces are supposedly "reality shows." He is the executive producer of The Real Housewives shows, about very expensive women living very expensive lives.

The first one started in Orange Country, California. The show has spread like cancer to New York, New Jersey, Beverly Hills, Miami, Dallas, Atlanta, Toronto, Athens, Melbourne.

What do these women do all day? Drink. Sit around the pool. Eat lunch. Fight. Wonder if they should inject Botox into their faces. Go on trips to resorts in Mexico. Buy more houses. Search for personal assistants. Visit Napa Valley. Go to male strip clubs. Spend $80,000 on a birthday party. Go to prison for financial fraud.

In other words, these people are among the most useless people on the planet. They do nothing for anyone else. They exist to be served.

I wonder what their carbon footprint is. How many tons of greenhouse gases are they helping to spew when they set up new multi-million houses or jet off to Puerto Rico?

I have an idea. Why doesn't Andy Cohen do a reality show on the Real Housewives of Rapid City, South Dakota, or the Real Housewives of the Bronx? Because he knows what sells. And while he says he selling reality, he's not really selling reality. He can't, and I suppose most television viewers can't, handle the reality of watching someone trying to make a living at a job that doesn't pay particularly well, or supporting your kids and making the rent or the mortgage payment every month.

The Real Housewives shows are aspirational marketing tools. Look at what these women have and what you don't have. Look at them drink. Look at them party. Look at them fly around the world. Wish I could do that. These shows are advertisements for all the consumer goods the TV housewives have.

You could have it all, like these ladies, if you looked right or worked hard or married the right guy, or were born somewhere else.

Andy Cohen has also created a number of reality shows, including Top Design, Make Me A Supermodel, Project Runway, Top Chef, The Millionaire Matchmaker, Million Dollar Listing (about super-expensive real estate), Tabitha's Salon Takeover, Being Bobby Brown, Flipping Out (about real estate and interior design and interpersonal turmoil) and Kathy Griffin – My Life on the D List.

He has been nominated for 18 Emmys. His Top Chef show won him an Emmy. He is extremely well-respected by the television industry.

The man hosts his own TV show on Bravo, a cable channel of NBC/Universal. He hosts various celebrities, from Mariah Carey to Ryan Seacrest and engages them in short discussions of what celebrities might be sleeping with what other celebrities, what celebrities are arguing with other celebrities, who was the most drunk at Kim and Kanye's wedding and so on. He asked Nick Jonas about spanking and foot fetishes. He asked Jason Priestly if he slept with Brad Pitt. He asked Susan Sarandon about her Twitter feud with Debra Messing. He asked Jennifer Lopez if she liked Ben Affleck's tattoo (she didn't).

Andy Cohen lives in celebrity world – a world of champagnes and fabulous parties and stunning interiors. He lives for pleasure-seeking and the glitzy company of world-famous entertainers.

Which is OK for him. The bigger problem is that millions of people want to be like him and his multitudes of housewives.

The vast wasteland just keeps getting bigger and Andy Cohen is the king of the junk culture trash heap. (Andy, here's a hot tip – do something positive for once. Plant a fucking tree or something.)

Are Andy Cohen's shows killing us? Not literally. But spiritually. And we're letting him.

Entertainment – Music

Music has been hijacked by the same corporate culture that dominates what we eat, what we wear, what we drive and what we see.

The music on the radio today is directed at sexual desire, nothing more. That makes it a tool of corporations that try to create and enhance your needs and wants to the point of buying their products.

I'll pick an easy example. Taylor Swift sings about running off with men, dating men whom she can't resist, all while wearing fashionably tight skirts and long dresses and red lipstick in the classic style, as she might sing it. She sings a lot about love that can never be attained, which is perfect, because that's what consuming is all about – reaching for something you can never really have.

Her album, titled "1989," for the year of her birth (1989 was incredibly consequential because that was the year she was born! We wouldn't want to say that the overthrow of Communist regimes in eastern Europe was as important as Taylor Swift being born.) is an ode to love, desire and expensive dresses. The video for "Wildest Dreams" could easily be a commercial for lipstick and every single piece of luxe clothing she wore.

The Hollywood Life web site said this about the video:

"Taylor Swift, you beautiful genius. The songstress, 25, debuted her Wildest Dreams music video during the MTV Video Music awards on Aug. 30 in LA, and the shoot is even more glam that we could have ever imagined – in fact, it just might be one of my fave Tay videos ever! Not only are we loving the romantic vibe, but the clothing is on the next level."

Following the article down the screen, Hollywood Life provides links to buy the same types of clothes Taylor likes, from crop tops to floral skirts so you can "rock the flirty trend like Taylor Swift."

It shouldn't surprise that Tay has a large endorsement deal with Diet Coke (Does this mean she'll pick up and recycle cans of Diet Coke thrown in the garbage? You would be doing the public a great service, Ms. Swift!). She's also a brand ambassador "for Target, Sony, Cover Girl and Elizabeth Arden," as the Huffington Post says (1/28/2013).

Swift has her own perfume, sold by Elizabeth Arden, called "Wonderstruck." The name of the perfume comes from her "Enchanted" song, "which reflected on the first impression one person has of another…The tagline for the fragrance is "The beginning of something magical."

So, this is how love and desire, music and advertising are now like multiple lovers intertwined. There are various brand extensions on the "Wonderstruck" perfume, including a body lotion, bath gel and a coin purse that "somewhat resembled the box that the perfume comes in," explains the TaylorSwift.wikia.com web site, a fan site.

The tagline for the commercial is, "Wonderstruck – the beginning of something magical." Hmm, sounds a little like Disney there. It's certainly magical to make the cash register sing.

Taylor Swift has a vision. It is a world where there is no pain and suffering other than her own romantic longings and nasty break-ups. But at least she has the money to buy nice clothes and make-up.

In the near future I expect Ms. Swift will release a song with a title something like, "You Are the Cherry Muffin Lipstick of My Soul."

Katy Perry's "Teenage Dream" song/video is a little less aspirational than Ms. Taylor Swift. She just wants a guy who's well-muscled with a three-day stubble of beard. (I wish one of these famous singers would create a video of longing for a boy who reads books, just once. That would be truly revolutionary.) The world in her video is the beach, freedom, fun and a very well-built man.

Rihanna's video, "We Found Love," focuses on Rihanna and her boyfriend tearing up the road in a too-fast Trans Am, smoking multiple cigarettes, playing the slots at the local casino, skateboarding, taking pills, drinking, shopping, stealing food from a little convenience store, screaming at each other, and possibly overdosing on drugs. One scene shows Rihanna slipping under the water of her bathtub as if to commit suicide. Nowhere is there any awareness that there is a world outside of themselves and their own immediate gratification.

In this video, Rihanna accidentally sheds insight into the insulated consumer world we live in – one defined by consuming quick thrills, enclosed in a gray palette of hopelessness because there's nothing bigger to live for.

Rihanna does have one song I found that speaks of a world greater than herself. It's called "World Peace." Some of the lyrics go like this:

"In a perfect world we would make love over war, with our hands in the air, got no problems, no care, oh no, Oh no!"

So, what's her solution to the problems? "We will dance in the rain despite all the pain." I find a slight cause for optimism in this line, because it acknowledges that there is injustice and sadness in the world.

Katy Perry has her own line of perfumes. She promotes Revlon Cover Girl nail gloss, lip gloss and make-up. Beyoncé has a $50 million deal to sell Pepsi. Rihanna has deals with Dior and Samsung. She sells a line of perfumes and also offers fragrances for men.

All these singers have successfully leveraged their singing popularity in the commercial world. They have made themselves into consumer products. You can't possibly be them, because there's only room for a few at the top, but you can try to buy a little piece of something they make or promote.

However, Rihanna surprised the hell out of me with her video, "American Oxygen," from 2015. The video is a stunning critique of the past and present of this country. On the one hand, it seems that Rihanna is praising the country with lyrics such as:

"Oh say can you see, this is the American Dream, young boy hustlin', tryna get the wheels in motion, but he can be anything at all, in America, America…"

On the other side of the optimism, I detected a faint whiff of class warfare in these lines:

"We sweat for a nickel and a dime, turn it into an empire."

Is she saying, people can work hard, but it won't make any difference to anyone but the government? I'm not sure.

The video rendition of the song is important. It shows immigrants trying to get to America, on ships and one the tops of trains. The immigrants also try to get over a Mexican border fence and are arrested. Another very quick shot features immigrants by the dozens taking the U.S. citizenship oath.

The film also shows power plants polluting the air with black smog, as Rihanna sings, "breathe in, American oxygen."

Watch the video and you'll see a homeless veteran asking for money on the street, an "Occupy Wall Street" protest, street riots, Fourth of July fireworks interspersed with burning buildings, presumably from riots, the Twin Towers being attacked, protests in Ferguson after Michael Brown was killed by police, even though he had no gun, protests against the death of Eric Garner in Staten Island (he was killed with a police choke hold), old film of the Ku Klux Klan riding on horses in the night, Muhammad Ali in his prime, practicing and prancing in the ring, a picture of the Lorraine Hotel, where Dr. Martin Luther King was shot and killed, a shot of Dr. King in his coffin, police beating African-American men, and a picture of sign that says, "We Owe Our Children A Just Society."

Rihanna also sings at the end of video, "This is the new America, we are the New America, with white and black kids sitting and playing together.

However, I'd take her more seriously if she wore a bra under her tee-shirt. Because that tells me the woman is selling her sexual desirability once again, even if the message is supposed to be serious. She's promoting the beauty of her upright breasts in the majority of the shots of her in the video.

In light of the police killings of Alton Sterling in Baton Rouge and Philando Castile in Minnesota and the killing of five police officers in Dallas in July, 2016, I hope Rihanna and other recording artists start singing more about social issues. Otherwise, I fear we'll be getting more "Bitch Better Have My Money" and "Teenage Dream."

As for the male side of the aisle, it's not much better. Beyond famous rapper Kanye West said Future's song, "March Madness" deserved consideration for a Grammy (Entertainment Weekly, 2/24/2016).

Let's look at some of the lyrics to the song here.

"All these cops shooting niggas, tragic, I'm the one that's living lavish, like I'm playing for the Mavericks, I didn't wanna fuck the bitch, the molly made me fuck her even though she average...dirty muddy in a cup, .45 by my gut...taking you out for some Jordans...Let's count this money, no rushin'. These fuckin' police can't touch me, These bogus police can't touch me."

Future spends one line on the dead men. The rest of it focuses on his money, his gun and his distaste for the woman he just slept with, blaming it on the MDMA, a form of methamphetamine, that he was taking at the time.

The guy seems talented, but the rest of the song looks like pretty much more of the same materialistic message and self-indulgent, self-centered thinking that we hear over and over again every day.

As far as his sponsor, Kanye West, composed this amazing song in 2004. Here are some of the lyrics:

"Getting choked by the detective yeah yeah now check the method, They be asking us questions, harass and arrest us... What's the basis?...God show me the way because the Devil trying to break me down (Jesus walks with me), The only thing that I pray is that my feet don't fail me now (Jesus walks), And I don't think there is nothing I can do now to right my wrongs (Jesus walks with me), I want to talk to God but I'm afraid because we ain't spoke in so long, To the hustlers, killers, murderers, drug dealers even the strippers (Jesus walks with them), To the victims of welfare for we living hell here hell yeah (Jesus walks with them)..."

Now, here's Kanye West in his 2016 video – "Famous":

"...I feel like me and Taylor might still have sex

Why? I made that bitch famous (God damn)

For all the girls that got d--ck from Kanye West

If you see 'em in the streets give 'em Kanye's best

Why? They mad they ain't famous (God damn)

They mad they're still nameless (Talk that talk, man) ..."

(West's 2016 argument with Taylor Swift about the lyrics and video to this song is a conversation that belongs to another world, yet which consumers seem to soak up – look at these famous people fighting! Yet, for all the words expended on this controversy, it has nothing to do with anyone else's day to day reality. This trivial excuse for a dispute just provides more meaningless fodder for the gossip-drenched media. It has no net effect on the lives of anyone outside of their families and employees. The two of them might as well be vomiting on each other on Neptune.)

The man who wrote the above lyrics signed a deal with Adidas to develop his own branded footwear and athletic shoes, clothes and accessories in the summer of 2016. A pair of his limited edition Air Yeezy brand shoes for Nike were sold on the Internet for close to $15,000 (source: CNN Money, 2/17/2015).

The limited edition strategy is very smart. It creates excitement about the product. It's exclusive. Less than 10,000 pairs might be produced. If you get a pair, you've obtained something your friends almost certainly don't have. A $350.00 shoe designed by one of the most famous rappers of all time.

What does this have to do with music? Nothing and everything. West has leveraged his music career into something completely different. The man who wrote

"Jesus Walks" is not just a rapper. He's a consumer product and a business man, further sad evidence of the commercialization of music.

Music is now almost completely a sub-discipline of advertising because it helps foster desires and a retail path to fulfill them, as opposed to a medium that offers the pleasure of words and music that combine to entertain and sometimes tell us something important about the world beyond our sight.

Let's contrast West with Marvin Gaye, who certainly sang about desire and sex, but who also sang these words:

"Mother, mother

There's too many of you crying

Brother, brother, brother,

There's far too many of you dying

You know we've got to find a way

To bring some lovin' here today – Ya

"Father, father

We don't need to escalate

You see, war is not the answer

For only love can conquer hate

You know we've got to find a way

To bring some lovin' here today

Picket lines and picket signs

Don't punish me with brutality

Talk to me, so you can see

Oh, what's going on...."

Gaye also sang these lyrics in 1971, the first time I ever heard anyone sing about pollution, in "Mercy Mercy Me":

"Woo ah, mercy mercy me,

Ah things ain't what they used to be, no no

Where did all the blue skies go?

Poison is the wind that blows from the north and south and east

Woo mercy, mercy me, mercy father

Ah things ain't what they used to be, no no

Oil wasted on the ocean and upon our seas, fish full of mercury

Ah oh mercy, mercy me

Ah things ain't what they used to be, no, no

Radiation underground and in the sky

Animals and birds who live nearby are dying…

What about this overcrowded land

How much more abuse from man can she stand…"

This song hit number one on the R & B charts and number four on the Billboard Pop chart (source: songfacts.com).

Gaye wasn't the only one. For example, Soundgarden, in Hands All Over, sang:

"Hands all over the coastal waters,

The crew men thank her

Then lay down their oily blanket

Hands all over the inland forest

In a striking motion trees fall down

Like dying soldiers."

The Pixies, in "Monkey Gone to Heaven," sang:

"…now there's a hole in the sky

And the ground's not cold

And if the ground's not cold

Everything is gonna burn."

Then there is the classic Joni Mitchell, who summed up the dilemmas of development and destruction in Big Yellow Taxi:

"Don't it always seem to go

That you don't know what you've got

Till it's gone

They paved paradise

And put up a parking lot."

Neil Young put this one up in 1989, in "Rockin' in the Free World," (source: azlyrics.com) which was just a little cynical about the George H.W. Bush administration, covering everything from drug use and homelessness to the ozone layer and guns:

"There's colors on the street

Red white and blue

People shufflin' their feet

People sleepin' in their shoes

But there's a warning sign

On the road ahead

There's a lot of people sayin'

We'd be better off dead

Don't feel like Satan,

But I am to them,

So I try to forget it,

Any way I can...

"I see a woman in the night

With a baby in her hand

Under an old street light

Near a garbage can

Now she puts the kid away,

And she's gonna get a hit,

She hates her life

And what she's done to it

There's one more kid

That will never go to school

Never get to fall in love,

Never get to be cool...

"We got a thousand points of light

For the homeless man

We got a kinder, gentler

Machine gun hand

We got department stores

And toilet paper

Got Styrofoam boxes

For the ozone layer,

Got a man of the people,

Says keep hope alive

Got fuel to burn,

Got roads to drive..."

The Beach Boys, of all people, musicians of eternal fun in the sun, even wrote a song about pollution, with these lyrics from "Don't Go Near the Water":

"Oceans, rivers, lakes and streams

Have all been touched by man

The poison floating out to sea

Now threatens life on land." (source for all environmental song lyrics: eia-international.org).

In our recent past, everyone from Elvis Costello ("What's So Funny About Peace, Love and Understanding") and Bruce Springsteen ("The River") to R.E.M ("Fall On Me") sang about social and environmental issues. John Mellencamp recorded the "The Authority Song," video, where the little people who bake the bread and fight the wars and clean the floors lose out to the rich business people every time.

Where are the singers and songwriters we need now to shout out about environmental and social issues today?

They're not on the radio stations most people listen to. Mainstream radio brings us Taylor Swift, Katy Perry and Miley Cyrus and soothing voices of rebellions only in style, urging us to go to the mall, buy some lipstick and find romance.

Consuming Beauty

As we have been trained to focus only on ourselves and not on helping something called "society," consumer products have increasingly targeted our minds for self-improvement in terms of both our looks and our behaviors.

Trista Sutter, a Midwestern woman, clean and pure, found love on ABC TV's "The Bachelorette" and got married in 2003, to a firefighter and former star college football player. She had a baby in 2007.

After her baby was born, Trista appeared on the cover of US Weekly, on a beach somewhere, wearing a yellow bikini and holding her baby in one hand. The magazine cover celebrated Trista's baby, but mostly it cheered her return to a bikini body.

The headlines and sub-headlines on the cover read:
- "How I Got My Body Back"
- "30 pounds in 5 months"
- "Fears She'd Never Be Sexy Again: 'I Was Hiding My Body'
- "Her Exact Diet and Workout"
- "Already Trying for Baby No. 2!"

When this issue of the magazine came out, I found the cover fascinating. I felt like Trista was saying to everybody:

"Look at my beautiful baby! No, look at my beautiful body! No, wait, sorry, look at the baby. Oh, I can't stand it! Please look at me. Look at me! My belly is flat. My breasts are large and well-rounded! I'm so happy I look sexy after this baby. Yes, look at the baby! But not too much. Because I'm here, and I look fantastic."

Consumerism has told us that we can have it all, which, let's face it, rarely happens. When it does happen, the news is actually surprising and we admire the people who have accomplished it. We want to live through the successful people and share in the glory they want to reflect on us.

Trista Sutter appears to be one of those people. She seems extremely nice. But her existence seems dedicated to having a good body, raising her babies and showing off to the world what a great life she has. She has her own web site. You can check her and her kids out anytime.

In 2012, Trista had plastic surgery to lift up her breasts and fix a drooping eye. The procedures were documented in Life & Style Weekly on August 5, 2012.

Here she is, talking about what she did and why she did it:

"'After nursing both my kids for a year each, my boobs were deflated,' mom of two Trista Sutter, 39, reveals exclusively in the new issue of Life & Style. 'And I had a droopy eye. It was something that I noticed in every picture I've ever taken.'

"After visits with her doctor...she decided to move forward with getting plastic surgery on her eyes and breasts – a blepharoplasty to lift her eyelids and remove the bags under her eyes, and breast augmentation with an internal lift that increased her cup size from a small B to a full C – all in one day," the online magazine article said.

"'I realized that the surgery was something I had to do for myself, just for my own self-confidence and to feel good again about being in bathing suits and being intimate with my husband,' Trista, who fell in love with her husband, Ryan... on The Bachelorette, in 2003, tells the mag.

"'`I wanted to feel pretty again – and I do!'"

Now, this is a lady who has a bachelor's degree in exercise science from Indiana University and master's degree in physical therapy from the University of Miami – pretty impressive. She provided kids with physical therapy over a four-year period at Miami Children's Hospital. She was also a dancer with the Miami Heat basketball team. She lives in Vail, Colorado, in the mountains, with her firefighter husband, who is also an endurance athlete in biking and running competitions. This guy is in great shape and he could probably beat me up in about two seconds.

Trista is also a woman who had her heart broken on national television (on "The Bachelor"), found a husband on "The Bachelorette" and got married in a ceremony recorded for broadcast to millions on ABC-TV. She also nearly died during her first pregnancy.

How do I know all this? It's on her web site, trista.sutter.com and in her book about gratitude, called "Happily Ever After – The Life Changing Power of a Grateful Heart". You can read the first pages of the book on Amazon.com, as I did.

She seems to have a beautiful life. You can look at pictures of her in the hospital with her newborn baby, at kids' birthday parties, smelling flowers with her children, hiking in the mountains, snowmobiling with her husband (try not to hurt the environment, there, kids!), looking fabulous in a dress for a night out with the husband, posing with her two dogs, visiting what look like vaguely famous people at concerts and athletic events, interviewing on "Good Morning America" and on and on. She clearly loves her children, her husband and her life.

She has her own collection of necklaces, photo frames, coffee mugs, refrigerator magnets, a foot-wide canvas that says "Be Grateful" and other domestic knick-knacks, sold under the brand name, "Grateful Heart."

As for the rest of us? We can admire this life of hers, but how many of us can really live like she does? How many of us can afford plastic surgery to fix the flaws too many of us obsess about, which we really shouldn't after all, because climate change is destroying our ability to live on the planet, among all the other little problems we face.

Trista Sutter is selling us dreams of living like her, but the most of any of us can really afford is to visit her web site, read about her in magazines, read her book about being grateful for what we've got and live through her vicariously. She represents aspirational marketing at its best. She sends out Instagram pictures of herself and her kids.

The point is that consumer culture has taught us to be self-centered. I don't think Trista Sutter is necessarily self-centered, but she sure does like to get photographed a lot.

(She obviously loves her kids, so maybe Trista would consider doing one more thing to help them have a good future – contribute money to environmental causes such as the Nature Conservancy, American Forests and the Environmental Defense Fund, and publicize what she's doing, to help persuade others who follow her on Instagram, Facebook and Twitter to do the same. She could use her fame to help make the case that we all need to do something to fight to prevent extreme climate change.)

As for the rest of the population, a lot of people want to be like Trista Sutter. Approximately five million women had undergone breast implant surgery by 2010 (source: www.pacificheightsplasticsurgery.com). In 2014, almost 300,000 women had the surgery. About one-third of the women were undergoing reconstruction after breast cancer (source: American Society of Plastic Surgeons).

About 18,000 women had buttocks augmentations in 2013 (source: www.cosmeticplasticsurgerystatistics.com), also known as the Brazilian butt lift, in which fat is added to your bottom, in an effort to make your behind look something like those belonging to Jennifer Lopez or Nicki Minaj.

Americans asked for and got from their plastic surgeons Botox injections, soft tissue fillers, chemical peels, laser hair removal, microdermabrasion (whatever that is), nose reshapings, eyelid surgery, liposuction to remove fat and facelifts.

Almost two million plastic surgery procedures were performed in 2015. Women paid $13.5 billion for them. The top five surgical procedures were the tummy tuck, the breast augmentation, the breast lift, eyelid surgery, not necessarily in that order (source: www.cosmeticplasticsurgerystatistics.com).

For nonsurgical procedures, Botox injection was the most popular, to try to minimize or get rid of wrinkles and facial creases. It works by blocking signals from the nerves to the muscles in your face, so the muscles can't contract.

Botox is an attempt to stave off the ravages of aging, I imagine. However, does it sound safe to screw around with your nervous system and your facial muscles? Botox can bruise your face (source: WebMd.com). Second, isn't aging inevitable anyway? If Cher can get old, then anybody can.

For those who don't want to get augmented, body improvements can be gained at the gym. Well, maybe.

Near where I work, there is a workout place that has a front window showing a giant photo of a woman with an abdomen that looks like she's ingested a small tank tread. Her face is tilted to the side and she has an arrogant look that says, "I'm an abdominal goddess. You want to look like this? I'll work you until you cry for Mommy."

Clearly, it's important to get in shape and stay in shape. But a lot of what we see in the media are young and wealthy people who devote their hours and days to working out intensively, with a highly expensive personal trainer – actors and actresses, for example.

Most people cannot possibly get to the stage of awesomeness that these people can achieve, which is part of the point. If it were easy, we would all have great bodies.

The bodies these young actors and actresses have is generally unreachable to the public, but we can dream of getting there eternally by buying exercise and health magazines, purchasing body building equipment that often isn't used and joining a health club. (And again, we see how the focus on the self takes over the mind space we ought to be devoting to the complex and myriad problems plaguing our world and how to do something positive to solve them.)

Here are some aspirational marketing samples from Fitness magazine:

- "Scarlett Johansson, 28, was able to rock a leather cat suit while filming The Avengers by doing loads of functional, power-building exercises. 'Scarlett really pushed herself with kettle ball (cast iron weights) moves, rope drills and weighted lunges,' says trainer Bobby Strom."
- "Alicia Keys' fave way to melt off more than 600 calories? An hour of high-octane kickboxing with trainer Jeanette Jenkins."
- "She's known for busting dance moves, but Britney Spears, 31, trained like an athlete to don those

curve-hugging minis for The X Factor. `We focus on...side shuffles while catching a medicine ball,' her trainer Derek DeGrazio says. He also makes her play this ab-carving game of toss: As Spears kneels about 20 feet away, DeGrazio rolls a medicine ball to her, which she picks up and throws back to him as hard as possible. `Then she drops onto her hands, does a modified push-up, gets up, and does it all over again,' DeGrazio says."

Here we see the ghost of aspirational marketing shadowing these stars. Shape magazine and Fitness magazine often have covers with Hollywood stars, such as Kaley Cuoco, Carrie Underwood, Sharon Stone, Isla Fisher and many other alpha females, with headlines that read:

- "Shed 10 lbs Fast"
- "Slim Down Fast"
- "Burn Fat Fast"
- "Best. Abs. Ever."
- "Sculpt Sexy Arms"
- "Hot Body"
- "Sizzle in Your Skinny Jeans"

The men are about the same in their messaging. From Men's Fitness and Muscle & Fitness magazines, we have seen:

- "Star Trek's Chris Pine – How He Got Ripped at Warp Speed!"
- "The Mark Wahlberg Way – Eat Smarter, Train Right, Dare to Win"
- "Build A Beach Body Like Chris Hemsworth"
- "4 Week Plan – BRAND NEW MUSCLE – Bigger Arms, Powerful Chest, Abs That Pop"
- "Melt Fat Fast! Lose Your Gut – 6 Weeks to Abs!"
- "Torch Fat! – 101 Ways to Get Ripped"

It's hard to do all this stuff. But, you can help yourself get there if you take steroids. Steroids give you a fast way to build muscles. They appeal to the consumer dream of building up your body fast and more easily.

Let's take, for example, Sylvester Stallone. I have followed this man's career from almost the very beginning. I loved the Rocky pictures. I've seen him in pictures you've never even heard of, such as "The Lords of Flatbush" "F.I.S.T" and "Paradise Alley." I even saw "Rocky V." (Rocky lost all his money and went to work as a boxing trainer, then he punched out the kid he was training, as well as a promoter who threatened to sue him. OK, never mind.) Anyone else see this movie? Raise your hands. I didn't think so.

Sylvester Stallone is as ripped as you can get, and he's aging into his seventies. How does he do it?

A blogger named Gareth Evans posted these comments on fitnessorstrength.com in 2014: "Due to overwhelming evidence, there is no questionable doubt that Sylvester Stallone uses anabolic steroids. For those of you who don't believe me, this includes a conviction in Australia for the possession of synthetic testosterone and the importation of human growth hormone (used to help build muscle)." (Stallone pleaded guilty in the case and paid a fine.)

"He looks great for his age, but much of his youth (muscle mass) is down to his vigilant use of drugs. It's extremely difficult to maintain a good level of muscle mass over 60, let alone keeping your body fat levels below 10 percent. One of the biggest causes of this is due to natural testosterone gradually dropping off as you get older. Many famous athletes, musicians and 'Hollywood' turn to private doctors to prescribe them with steroids/HGH to combat false 'medical' conditions (such as AIDS or muscular dystrophy) or simply 'anti-aging' to allow them to legally take the drugs. However, in many cases they are supervised by doctors, but the drugs they take are completely illegal," Evans wrote.

What are the negatives of using steroids and HGH?

Steroids first. They are artificially made creations similar in chemical composition to testosterone. They will make your muscles bigger and stronger, states the Web.MD web site. "Anabolic steroids may be taken as a pill, as a shot into a muscle, or as a gel or cream rubbed on the skin," the site says.

These products can give you high blood pressure or cause a heart attack or stroke. They might cause liver disease and liver cancer, especially if you take steroid pills. Your liver needs to metabolize the pill when you digest it, so the steroid can hurt the liver. The drug may also cause rage, aggression, violence, mania and delusions (source: WebMD.com).

On synthetic HGH, Web MD states that this product is often used legitimately if your body does not produce enough of it naturally. It "spurs growth in children and adolescents. It also helps to regulate body composition, body fluids, muscle and bone growth, sugar and fat metabolism and possibly heart function."

Weight lifters like HGH because it can increase muscle size and metabolism (source: bodybuilding.com). WebMD states that HGH can "regulate body composition, body fluids, muscle and bone growth, sugar and fat metabolism and possibly heart function."

Using and abusing HGH might cause you to suffer nerve, muscle or joint pain, body tissue swelling, carpal tunnel syndrome, high cholesterol and numbness or tingling on your skin, diabetes and the growth of cancerous tumors (source: WebMD.com).

Also, sports heroes contribute their share in the unofficial marketing of these steroids by simply performing in a game. Alex Rodriguez, the Yankees star, was banned from baseball for a year for juicing. Lance Armstrong, who won the Tour De France bike race seven times, took steroids. The list is long and depressing, including Barry Bonds, Mark McGwire, Sammy Sosa, Ryan Braun and Hulk Hogan.

Sylvester Stallone can do whatever he wants with his body. However, like many Hollywood stars, his body is a walking advertisement. Naturally, there are legions of teenage boys who want to get as ripped as Stallone or their favorite Hollywood icon or sports star, in as little time as possible, which is the consumer way.

One of every 20 teenagers is taking steroids to increase muscle mass (source: Mayo Clinic). It would be interesting to do a study of how many of these kids also drink Red Bull and other energy drinks.

In 2010 there were approximately 22 million boys and girls aged 15 to 19 years old in the U.S. (source: U.S. Census data). So, if one in every 20 teens is taking steroids, that works out to be about one million kids. Not just boys are taking steroids. Some girls are too. They're doing it to tone their bodies and reduce fat (source: drugfree.org/Partnership for a Drug-Free America, 7/22/2014).

Also, 11 percent of teens in high school – ninth grade through 12th -- are reportedly using HGH (source: drugfree.org). Why are they taking it? To get stronger, more muscular, thinner or improve their athletic abilities (source: hgh10.com).

About steroids, the site stated: "'With young women, you see them using it more as a weight control and body-fat reduction method,' said Jeff Hoerger, of Rutgers University, who has recently counseled two young girls who had used steroids – one an 11th-grade swimmer who wanted help with weight loss. 'She was just looking for quick results,' Hoerger said."

Quick results. We've all been trained to expect quick results. Consumer culture is doing this to us. We're hooked on a dream and it's malign one – that we must sculpt our bodies to the level of Hollywood and professional sports. In the process, we may damage our bodies in such a way as to endanger our lives.

Here is the irony of consumer culture in steroid use and abuse – we want to make ourselves look better, to make ourselves healthier than we currently are, and in the process we are hurting our health in a serious and potentially lasting way. The dream revealed is a nightmare.

Gambling as Consuming

Gambling is the ultimate consumer snakebite.

If you can't be as rich as a pop star, because your job pays you by the hour, you can try your hand at the casino. For one quarter, you can pull the lever and make a lot of money.

That's the promise.

Gambling really means turning yourself into an unthinking zombie in search of the big hit. It convinces you that you can defy the long odds of winning, where all others have failed. In a sense you're asking the universe to help you win.

Slot machines are the most popular form of gambling now (source: Vox.com, 3/1/2015). They're easy and don't require bluffing, like in poker, or learning how to play a table game, like Blackjack. All you have to do is pull the lever.

I went with my parents once to the Mohegan Sun casino in Connecticut. I was an adult, already in my fifties, and visiting them at their summer apartment in a beautiful country town in northeastern Connecticut. They used to come up north in the summer to escape the Florida heat.

My parents really wanted to go and I said OK. The only thing they wanted to play was the slots. My father and mother walked around the casino, each with a cup of quarters. There were dozens of other elderly people there, dunking their money in the machines and hoping for a hit. My father won several times over the few hours we were there, so he told me I was his good luck. I think he won $20.00. How much he and my mother put in the machines I can't say. We used the "winnings" to buy lunch at a casino restaurant near the slot machines.

My father was not alone in his superstitions. Many other people treat the machine as something that it isn't. They're hoping for a lucky break from the machine.

The machine does not think in terms of lucky breaks.

"It is true that a slot machine is designed to average a certain payout percentage over millions of spins, but that's millions of spins. No payouts or lack thereof will affect the short-term odds of winning...So they next time you're walking through a room full of slot machines and see a man tapping the screen with one hand, covering his eyes with the other and murmuring softly, remember: The slot machine doesn't hear you, and doesn't care. It'll pay you when it's good and ready (source: mlive.com).

There are millions of people walking around looking to play slot machines.

The casino closest to my house is the Empire City Casino in Yonkers. It has more than 5,000 slot machine games, from "Sex and the City" to "Michael Jackson King of Pop" and "NASCAR". The Resorts World casino in Queens, at the Aqueduct race track has 3,000 slots.

There are casinos in 43 of the 50 states of the union. Now of course we also have online gambling.

How did our gamblers do?

"The gambling industry around the world is huge, but the biggest market is the United States, where the biggest market is the United States, where gamblers lost a staggering $119 billion in 2013 (source: The Week magazine, 2/5/2014).

The promise of winning at gambling is obviously a con. This is income transfer on an enormous scale, from the lower and middle classes to the rich. Who are the winners here? Let's identify some of them.

Frank and Lorenzo Fertitta own Station Casinos, a company which operates 14 casinos in the Las Vegas area (source: University of Nevada/Las Vegas Center for Gaming Research). Frank is worth about $1.59 billion (source: Forbes.com) and Lorenzo about $2 billion (source: celebrity networth.com). The brothers operated the Ultimate Fighting Championship (UFC), which knocked us out in the Advertising – Eating and Drinking Chapter earlier in this book. The Fertittas sold the UFC for $4 billion in 2016.

Steve Wynn owns the Mirage, Bellagio, Treasure Island and Wynn Las Vegas. He's worth about $2.8 billion (source: Forbes magazine).

Sheldon Adelson has a reported net worth of $23 billion (source: therichest.com). He owns the Las Vegas Sands Corporation, which includes The Venetian, the Palazzo, the Sands Expo and the Sands Bethlehem (Pennsylvania). He also owns several gaming properties in Macao, an autonomous territory in the Pearl River Delta bordering China (source: Las Vegas Sands Corp.).

Steven Wynn generally gives money to Republican Party causes and candidates (source: Associated Press, 10/13/2015). Sheldon Adelson also gives money to the Republican Party – lots of it, which we'll get to in a minute.

So, anyone who gambles in the casinos of Wynn and Adelson is basically just giving money to the Republican Party to fund candidates who will enact government policies that will almost certainly hurt the patrons of these establishments. So, they lose twice. The rest of us lose only once, but we lose BIG.

ProPublica, a nonprofit journalism organization (12/20/2012), investigated Adelson's political contributions. Its reporters found that Adelson and his wife gave $98 million in 2012 to a number of Republican candidates (source: ProPublica news story, 12/20/2012). They gave about $30 million to a political action committee trying to elect Mitt Romney President. The rest went to various Republican Congressional and Senate candidates across the country.

That's not all of it. ProPublica reported that Adelson contributed so called "dark money," to various conservative political groups that don't have to report who their donors are. The Supreme Court's Citizens United decision (a 5-4 decision, like Bush vs. Gore in 2000) let loose a flood of "unlimited corporate and union giving." In the ProPublica article, the reporters cited a Huffington Post estimate that Adelson may have given conservative PACs another $50 million in funds to elect Republican candidates.

That's how gambling works. You put your money in the mouth of the machine and a Republican Party Senator or Representative, and possibly a President, comes out the other end.

State lotteries in 43 states took in almost $74 billion in 2015 (source: statista.com). While state lotteries are devoted to funding government programs, they are a regressive tax on the poor.

The Journalist Resource project at Harvard citing a paper in the Journal of Gambling Studies, stated that "the poor are still the leading patron of the lottery and even the people who were made to feel poor buy lotteries."

The legalized gambling that comprises state lottery systems is helping to create a population of people who find it normal to gamble. "...other studies, such as 2010 paper in the Journal of Community Psychology, find that lottery outlets are often clustered in neighborhoods with large numbers of minorities, who are at the greatest risk for developing gambling addiction," the Journalist Resource project article stated.

In this paragraph, we have the promise of gambling laid bare. It's a consumer con, promising riches to those who can least afford to buy the ticket. Lotteries feed the appetite for luxury goods without ever satiating it. It therefore inspires gamblers to gamble more. It's a shallow, vacuous dream.

Also, playing the lottery may possibly act as a bridge to other games of chance (but really, what chance does any of us really have in that situation?), introducing people to the idea of finding other places to gamble, like a casino. Great, huh?

Does playing the lottery lead to gambling addiction?

The New York Times worked with Dr. Timothy Fong, co-director of the gambling studies program and associate professor of psychiatry at UCLA to help answer the question.

As quoted in the Times online blog on 11/4/2010, Dr. Fong said, "There is no scientific data that I have seen that shows that lottery play can lead directly to gambling addiction. Playing the lottery is still gambling, though, so lottery games that offer a high reward with high frequency – for example, 'scratch' games or video lottery terminals – probably carry a higher chance of harm."

On the blog, Dr. Fong also said: "The pace of gambling has proceeded faster than our ability to understand its direct impact on individuals, family and society. The gambling industry understands that its product is addictive, and it has taken steps to reduce the harm."

The gambling magnates Wynn and Adelson and state governments across the country have figured out how to talk to the most vulnerable among us and draw them in with colored lights and tickets, buzzing sounds and bells, and not least, fantasies of getting rich without really working for it. They are no better than carnival barkers.

Gambling is the perfect consumer product because you rarely, if ever, get to see, feel, or touch the product you want to buy. What the gambler gets is a long parade of chances they buy, with the payoffs receding farther and farther away from them.

Like the social, health and environmental problems brought on by purchasing everything from Coca-Cola to off-road vehicles, gambling creates enormous problems for addicts and those around them. In other words, the producer makes the money while the rest of us often end up paying for the problems associated with using the product

"Compulsive gambling accounts for as much as five billion dollars spent annually in the United States alone," explains the website Addictions.com. "Many of the people who are addicted to gambling find themselves accruing tens or hundreds of thousands of dollars in debt."

"The negative effects of problem gambling include: financial problems, including high debt, poverty or bankruptcy, domestic violence and child abuse in families, suicidal thoughts, actions or actually committing suicide, legal troubles, including arrests for theft or prostitution and "behavior problems in children of problem gamblers."

Gambling on the lottery or at the casino creates potential problems for everybody.

"The weight of the empirical evidence suggests that casinos do in fact impose negative social costs on surrounding communities, notably, an increased prevalence of property and violent crime," states the Brookings Institution in a 2005 research paper (source:

http://www.brookings.edu/views/papers/200502kearney.pdf).

The paper also addresses the cost of lottery tickets. "Does spending on lottery tickets crowd out savings and consumption, or merely other forms of gambling. Analyzing multiple sources of micro-level data…finds that household lottery spending is financed entirely by a reduction in non-gambling expenditures."

So, it's possible that the kids might not get the milk they need because Dad just spent money on playing the new scratch off game.

When I walk into my neighborhood stationery store, the one with the 5-Hour Energy Drink on the counter, I can also see the lottery video boards hanging from the ceiling. Men and women come in and buy the tickets constantly. I don't see many winners in there. But still they try, every day.

At this point, I question whether it's even accurate to call the place a stationery store. It's really a gambling parlor that also sells greeting cards and newspapers. And, conveniently, there's one in every neighborhood in my city.

Shareholder Value Is Just Another Way to Say Give Me More Money

The new "It" phrase that's thrown around a lot these days is "shareholder value." What this phrase means in practice is that the people who own the company can slash employees, send jobs overseas at will and pollute our common resources, with only one goal in mind – to enrich the owners no matter how wealthy they already are.

Shareholder value is defined by the web site Investopedia as: "...the value delivered to shareholders because of management's ability to grow sales, earnings and free cash flow over time. A company's shareholder value depends on strategic decisions made by senior management, including the ability to make wise investments and generate a healthy return on invested capital. If this value is created over the long term, the share price increases and the company can pay larger cash dividends to shareholders."

Let's find an example of shareholder value in action.

United Technologies' (UTC)Carrier Corporation announced plans in early 2016 to move 2,100 jobs in Indiana to Mexico. The jobs being moved pay about $20.00 per hour.

The Mexican workers who will do these jobs, starting in 2017, will get paid about $3.00 an hour (source: New York Times, 3/19/2016).

United Technologies had sales of $56 billion in 2015. Its net income was approximately $4 billion. That's the pure profit the company earned, after expenses and taxes were paid.

Gregory Hayes is the current CEO of United Technologies. His current salary, not including bonuses is approximately $1.3 million yearly (source: asyousow.org).

One million to run a giant conglomerate doesn't sound so awful. But his predecessor is something else.

In late 2014, Hayes' predecessor, Louis Chenevert, left the corporation with a retirement package worth more than $195 million, including company stock, options and pension benefits (source: Fortune.com, 2/6/2015).

Chenevert received $136 million in stock options, almost $31 million in pension benefits and "$27.9 million in stock tied to the company's performance," Fortune stated.

Here's the thing about shareholder value. Corporate honchos like to trot it out when they have to cut jobs. But when it comes to the people who lead the corporation this phrase magically does not appear in anyone's statements. The Indiana workers' jobs are being cut and Chenevert, who will be doing nothing to help the corporation from now on, as well as other stockholders, will receive the money that could have gone to the people who actually make the products the corporation sells.

But, shareholder value demands that average hourly wages go down from $20.00 to $3.00, via Carrier's Mexico strategy, right?

It's Robin Hood in reverse.

Let's look a little more closely at the man who will receive some of the benefits of the move to Mexico. Chenevert may have been forced out of the company because of an incident with his yacht.

"United Technologies' board was reportedly unhappy with Chenevert after he took a side trip to Taiwan during a business trip to check on the construction of his yacht." (Why wasn't the yacht being built by American workers in the U.S.? Too expensive for this multi-millionaire?)

"The board confronted Chenevert about the trip and his priorities just prior to his retirement, according to a Wall

Street Journal article in December that cited anonymous sources," The Fortune article stated.

The Wall Street Journal (WSJ, 12/5/2014) described Chenevert's yacht: "The new vessel, a 110-foot-long P110, is being customized for Ms. Chenevert, the person said. The standard model can accommodate between 16 and 20 passengers, features an enclosed 'sky lounge' about the main deck and is powered by twin 1,600 horsepower Caterpillar engines."

Thank you to the Wall Street Journal for discovering and disclosing these choice details:

"Top managers at the industrial units of United Technologies, which manufactures Pratt & Whitney jet engines, Sikorsky helicopters, Otis elevators and Carrier air conditioning units, complained that they were having difficulty getting adequate access to the CEO when they needed it...

"Mr. Chenevert bought a 63-foot Hatteras motor yacht in 2003. He sold it after he had a new 85-foot vessel custom built...at a factory in...Taiwan...Mr. Chenevert sold his second yacht last year after listing it for $3.3 million and is having a new, bigger one built...at the same factory. Mr. Chenevert stopped there to check in on the yacht's progress from Nov. 10 to Nov. 12, a person familiar with the matter said."

So, here's a guy who spent three days watching and supervising the building of his yacht while ignoring his responsibilities at his enormous company, with close to 200,000 employees. His priorities were just a little (just a little!) mixed up and he wasn't focused on the company's business. And he walks away with $195 million. But the workers in Indiana get fired. And Louis Chenevert gets to cavort in the waves and pollute the air and water with the gross quantities emitting from his monster boat. This is another, but more horrifying, example of "let me enjoy nature while I destroy it." Somebody needs to calculate this guy's carbon footprint and publicize it.

I am arguing that the ideas behind shareholder value and excessive CEO pay packages are simply the extension of consumer culture ideas of instant gratification and selfishness to higher and higher levels, far beyond what many people previously thought possible.

We've all been trained by television, radio, the Internet and all other forms of mass communication to want more stuff. Louis Chenevert has proved himself better at it than most. The vast majority of CEOs and other people in the public eye have accomplished the same thing.

Of course, successful people deserve to make more money. But the drive to succeed becomes increasingly and excessively warped when people act as if getting and spending more is all that's worth pursuing in life, to the exclusion of all other values.

Activist investor Carl Icahn presents an example of how the term "shareholder value" can distort corporate management and turn businesses into instant gratification machines.

"Carl Icahn has amassed a 7.77 percent stake in Manitowoc," a Wisconsin manufacturer of cranes and food service equipment, according to Fortune magazine's December 29th, 2014 issue.

Icahn made his investment in order to complain about it. "Calling the shares 'undervalued,'" Icahn said he would discuss such possible moves" (such as splitting up the company), "with Manitowoc's management and board of directors and could also seek board representation...Icahn has acquired 10.5 million shares at a cost of about $146.6 million, according to a filing with the Securities and Exchange Commission."

Icahn thinks he's doing a good thing. As his web site puts it, "...Carl Icahn's efforts have unlocked billions of dollars of shareholder and bondholder value and have improved the competitiveness of American companies. He and his affiliated companies currently own businesses in a wide range of industries, including real estate, telecommunications, transportation, industrial services, oil refining and manufacturing."

The man has a net worth of $18 billion (source: celebritynetworth.com) and doesn't believe he's part of the establishment, according to a video on his web site. As I write this words, it's the summer of 2016 and Donald Trump has just been nominated by the Republican Party to be President of the United States.

In Icahn's "Danger Ahead" video on his web site, he said he supported Donald Trump for President because "he will shake things up and "move Congress" to do something. Trump is on record as wanting to pass a bill for large tax cuts, which would give even more money to the wealthiest among us. Is that what Icahn wants? Does Icahn really need more money?

In late 2015, Icahn threatened to spend $150 million to defeat for re-election legislators in the House of Representatives who didn't vote for a tax cut on corporations' overseas profits (source:movetoamend.org).

Corporations in the U.S. have parked about $2 trillion (you read that correctly) in off shore bank accounts. Icahn wants to cut tax rates on the money and "let them bring that money home at a massive tax discount," the writer Paul Blumenthal says on the movetoamend.org web site.

"Coincidentally, Icahn is one of the largest investors in Apple, which holds over $181 billion in profits overseas – more than any other U.S. multinational corporation," Blumenthal writes.

This is a coincidence? Oh, and by the way, if you can spend $150 million on politics you are very much part of the establishment.

"This really sums up what politics has come to be, which is an argument among billionaires,' said Nick Nyhart, president and CEO of Every Voice Center, which advocates for campaign finance reform," stated the movetoamend.com article.

So, again, as in the case of people who gamble at Sheldon Adelson's or Steve Wynn's casinos, whenever you buy an iPhone or iPod, or other Apple products, you are giving people like Carl Icahn money to "persuade" Congress to enrich himself, possibly at your expense.

Some people don't believe that Carl Icahn has corporations' best interests at heart when he buys their shares. Witness another CEO on Icahn's move against Mantiwoc:

"When corporate raider Carl Icahn pontificates about 'shareholder value,' let's be clear he isn't talking about building long-term value by building useful goods and services. He is talking about making a trading profit in the very short term," states John Torinus, chairman of a privately-owned graphic parts manufacturer in Wisconsin, who has his own web site (johntorinus.com).

"Icahn's push for a break-up at Manitowoc is his standard gimmick. His formula involves splitting off divisions with little regard to long-term consequences," Torinus says. It sounds like Icahn has fully ingested the consumer culture value of instant gratification and getting what you want whether you hurt anyone else or not.

"Expect Icahn...to move out of the two stocks" (if the company splits up) "in relatively short order once they make a trading profit. He has no fundamental interest in what the company does in the real world, like build good products."

Torinus continues: "There are some corporations that need a shake-up from outside investors and that can work if the new investors put their money in for the long pull. Other stakeholders like employees, customers, vendors, communities, lenders and governments come out ahead when there is a long-term commitment."

Making a long-term commitment is the exact opposite of what the consumer culture dictates. Icahn presents himself at a savior of "undervalued corporations." He's not. He's there to pull as much money out of any given public company as he can.

In contrast to Icahn's presentation of himself as doing good work, Torinus says, "It's hard to figure why Icahn does what he does...Maybe he just likes playing the game.

That's what it is to him, a game. But it's not a game to the many people who put their lives into his target companies."

Torinus is a real, if unknown, revolutionary against consumer culture. He has strong roots in the Wisconsin community. He served in the U.S. Marines. He is the chairman of the Wisconsin state chapter of the Nature Conservancy, which buys land and preserves natural habitats for animals. He helps fledgling entrepreneurs build their businesses.

Contrast Torinus with Icahn. In 1985, Icahn more or less single-handedly obliterated Trans World Airlines (source; Milwaukee Journal Sentinel 2/9/2015 edition of www.jsonline.com). He took over the company, then took it private. TWA was left with about $540 million in debt. Icahn picked up $469 million in "personal profit." Then he "sold TWA's London routes to American Airlines in 1991 for $445 million," the Journal Sentinel article states.

I wonder, how many thousands of TWA employees lost their jobs because of what Icahn did.

And how is Icahn doing? He owns an estate in East Hampton and apartment on Fifth Avenue in Manhattan. His 178-foot yacht, called "Starfire," is worth approximately $37.5 million (source: bornrich.com). He likes to drink martinis.

Michael Dell, CEO and founder of the Dell, Inc. computer company, gave $250,000 to the Republican Party to help elect George W. Bush President (source: www.knowthecandidates.com). He probably has a personal carbon footprint that's the size of Saudi Arabia. Michael Dell is not my kind of guy.

However, in contrast to Icahn, Dell has created a company that actually makes real products.

Icahn wanted to buy Dell's company in 2013 (source: theverge.com). This is his opinion of Icahn:

Dell said: "He lies, he has no ethical boundaries, he'll say anything, do anything, I have no time for him (source: www.crn.com)." Dell took the company private, over Icahn's objections. But Dell's move got his company out of the craziness of the stock market.

Like Icahn, Wall Street in general long ago bought into the fever of gross consumption and spreads it with every breath. Unfortunately, Icahn is part of a crowd that possesses gnawing appetites for cash and lives for the thrill of the moment. They live and die with quarterly earnings. That's the length of their attention span – three months. Cash is food for them, and the more they get the better, and as fast as possible. They're not too interested in investing for the future.

Wall Street culture is consumer culture on methamphetamines, and it's what gave us the 2007-2008 housing crash and the Great Recession that followed, which was so much fun for all of us.

The only personal window I ever got into this kind of Wall Street fever is to tell a story about one of the wealthiest people I ever personally knew. I went to a state university in upstate New York with this guy. We had rooms on the same floor of our dorm my sophomore year. A very nice guy and very ethical.

He ended up running a very successful company. The last time I saw him he told me he played golf two or three times a week. Also, he had just recently purchased a very expensive home. He showed me a photo of the house on his iPhone. The house looked like it cost anywhere from $3 to $5 million.

Then we moved the conversation onto politics. My friend wanted more Republicans in Congress and a Republican in the White House (except for Trump – he said he wouldn't vote for Trump), so he could get lower tax rates (this was January, 2016 and each party's Presidential debates were already on television). Whatever he was earning wasn't enough for him.

I asked him what he wanted. He said just one word: "More."

The one question I should have asked him next is "Why?"

Consuming Politics

American politics has become a supermarket. The only real buyers, though, the ones who actually matter, are the super-rich who can afford to spend seemingly limitless amounts of money on getting the politicians and laws they want. The rest of us are effectively shut out of the system. The people and companies with the most money get the luxury service they think they deserve.

Problem is, our government is not supposed to be a supermarket for the super-rich.

Whatever these people and corporations want, it's never enough. They keep coming for seconds, thirds, fourths and so on. They have proven to be excellent consumers, who want only what's best for themselves and forget everyone else.

Here are some examples of what big corporations have purchased with their contributions to political campaigns and super PACs (political action committees).

The oil and gas industry receives approximately $41 billion in tax breaks every year (source: Christian Science Monitor, 3/9/2011).

How can this happen when the oil and gas business is extremely profitable and conservative lawmakers are braying that we must cut the deficit and national debt? And what about the carbon pollution these companies spew, at no cost to themselves, but to the American public? We pay for their pollution, with high asthma rates, lung diseases and other health problems, as well as the awful price we will all expend on dealing with a hotter climate.

It's pretty simple. The oil and gas companies have purchased the services of the United States government by giving our representatives and senators lots of money. Since 1990, the industry has given "more than $357 million" to candidates for Federal office. The oil and gas industry bought themselves people who will keep the Federal tax breaks coming. Four of five dollars the industry spent went to Republicans running for office (source: motherjones.com).

Farmers get about $20 billion a year in subsidies from the Federal government (source: The Economist, 2/14/2015). And we're not talking about little Farmer Jones who has a small wheat field and works the field himself to grow his crop.

Here's a partial list of the 50 billionaires who have received farm subsidies: Charles Schwab, the owner of the Charles Schwab & Co., the big discount investor, who has a net worth of about $5 billion. Also getting farm subsidies are: Paul Allen, who co-founded Microsoft and is worth $15 billion, Anne Walton Kroenke, a Wal-Mart family heir, worth about $4.5 billion and David Rockefeller, Sr., a Rockefeller family heir who is worth about $3 billion. Leslie Wexner, Chairman and CEO of L Brands, which owns Victoria Secret and Bath and Body Works, who has a net worth of about $7.6 billion (source: Environmental Working Group's AgMag, 4/18/2016).

The agribusiness lobby gave $67 million to politicians in 2015-2016. Three quarters of their contributions were given to members of the Republican Party (source: opensecrets.org/Center for Responsive Politics). Is there a relationship between the giving of the money and the receiving of the subsidies?

It's hard to find anything definitive online about the relationship between campaign contributions and farm subsidies, but the money keeps flowing to the politicians and the subsidies keep coming to billionaires.

There are many other areas where the agriculture industry is getting a lot of return for its political spending. This sector includes farming, sugar cane growers and processors, livestock and meat, poultry and egg producers, dairy farmers, logging companies, tobacco crops and food processors and grocery companies.

U.S. Sugar is a Florida-based grower of sugar cane, citrus and sweet corn. U.S. Sugar produces 10 percent of all the sugar made in the U.S. (source: U.S. Sugar.com). American Crystal Sugar, another producer, sells sugar to candy and chocolate manufacturers, breakfast cereal makers and bakeries (source: www.crystalsugar.com). Florida Crystals is a major sugar producer as well.

U.S. Sugar and Florida Crystals each gave politicians and PACs about $900,000 in 2015 and 2016. American Crystal Sugar gave almost $2 million, during the same period (source: Center for Responsive Politics).

What do these and other sugar growers get in return? In 2013, they got about $300 million for their spending (source: Americans for Tax Reform).

Americans for Tax Reform (ATR), a conservative policy group led by Grover Norquist, who famously promised to shrink government to the point where he could drown it in a bathtub, and with whom I agree on almost nothing else, has pointed out that the sugar program is very expensive for the American taxpayer.

"...the sugar program has led to billions of their hard earned dollars being wasted propping up the sugar industry. In 2013, nearly $300 million was charged to taxpayers by the program, and the Congressional Budget Office projects the program will cost taxpayers an additional $115 million over the next 10 years," the ATR website says.

Marco Rubio, the Senator from the Florida Crystals company, oops, I mean the state of Florida, who ran for President in 2016, received $114,000 in 2013-2014 from the family that controls Florida Crystals. Florida Crystals also gave Rubio $371,000 for his Presidential campaign.

Florida's Lake Okeechobee, St. Lucie River and Indian River Lagoon are all connected. The water from the lake flows into the river and the lagoon, then the Atlantic Ocean. The water from the lake is polluted with agricultural runoff – much of it fertilizer from sugarcane plantations (source: Earthjustice, an environmental group).

"Billions of gallons of polluted water are pumped off the sugar cane fields...The flow from the pumping station creates a highly visible 'plume'...This plume contains high levels of phosphorous and nitrogen along with high levels of dissolved organic materials that come from agricultural and urban wastes (sewage)," Earthjustice says.

The pollution creates giant blooms of algae, which starve the water of oxygen and turns the water into poison for humans and animals alike.

"Because of this excessive fertilization, the Lake (Okeechobee) now chronically suffers from toxic blue-green algae blooms...Blue-green algae toxins can affect the liver, nervous system and skin, and have been linked to increases in liver cancer...skin rashes, abdominal cramps, nausea...and vomiting. Numerous dog and cattle deaths have been attributed to toxic algae," the Earthjustice report says.

"Sixty percent of the plant life has died off. Manatees and dolphins are dying at an alarming rate," stated The Daily Beast online web site on 3/14/2016.

Rubio's response? Nothing.

Why? Is Rubio's lack of response due to his connection to Florida Crystals?

"Florida Crystals has...opposed multiple attempts by the state of Florida to buy the land south of Lake Okeechobee to relieve water releases into the Indian River Lagoon," stated the Daily Beast article. "That land has long been used to farm sugar."

Let's look at Mitch McConnell, U.S. Senator from Kentucky. He received about $1.2 million from the oil and gas industry from 2011 to 2016, according to the Center for Responsive Politics. So it's very convenient for him to deny climate change (source: Huffington Post, 10/3/2014). McConnell consistently votes against regulating carbon and water pollution as well as protecting habitat (source: League of Conservation Voters).

James Inhofe, Senator from Oklahoma, a loud climate change denier, received about $600,000 from the oil and gas industry, coal mining interests and electric utilities from 2009 to 2014. Inhofe voted against regulations to limit carbon pollution (source: League of Conservation Voters).

Lamar Smith, a U.S. Representative from Texas, took in almost $76,000 from the oil and gas industry from 2011 to 2016. He's another prominent climate change denier. Smith voted to bar the Environmental Protection Agency from regulating greenhouse gases, voted no to limit carbon pollution and voted to end subsidies for clean energy industries such as solar and wind. He also voted to open up the continental shelf for oil drilling (source: ontheissues.org).

Chuck Schumer, Senator from New York, got about $3 million from the securities and investment industry, from 2011 to 2016. Senator Schumer serves on the Banking, Housing and Urban Affairs Committee and the Finance Committee in the Senate.

Whatever a Senator's personal beliefs, who doesn't believe there is a connection between the money our Congress members receive from particular industries and their votes in Congress? If I was a Senator and I received a $50,000 gift from the oil and gas industry, I would certainly think how my vote might affect the way I feel about the group that gave me the gift.

Our business sector treats our Senators and Representatives, whom we pay with our tax dollars, as consumer products. If business buys them, they stay bought, like a product is supposed to be.

Fortunately, you can find out some information on who is giving money to whom. To learn the facts on what organizations are donating to your Representative or Senator, go to opensecrets.org, a web site operated by the Center for Responsive Politics, which tracks the money spent on politics "and its effect on elections and public policy."

Wealthy individuals, who are the biggest owners of the businesses we're talking about, also generally treat Congress as a market and they buy people who agree with them on taxes.

The sainted Ronald Reagan started this trend. His sunny optimism sold tax cuts for the rich and the rich have been going downhill in terms of moral obligation to the country ever since.

Reagan's tax cuts and policies resulted in a drastic increase in taxes on high-income taxpayers. Tax rates on the wealthy went from 70 percent to 28 percent (source: CNN.com).

The idea behind the tax cuts was something called "supply-side economics." The theory went that tax cuts for the rich would free up more money for investment, which would trickle down to the rest of us.

"Tax relief for the rich would enable them to spend and invest more. This new spending would stimulate the economy and create new jobs. Reagan believed that a tax cut of this nature would ultimately generate even more revenue for the federal government," stated ushistory.org, a non-partisan web site. Reagan also increased military spending by $100 billion a year (source: thinkprogress.org) and busted the Federal budget. The national debt tripled under Reagan, from one trillion to three trillion dollars (source: ushistory.org).

As President, Reagan asked for a balanced budget amendment to the Constitution (easier said than done!), which would help discipline the spending spree he himself had helped initiate. I characterize the balanced budget amendment idea from conservatives as "Stop me before I spend again."

And spend Reagan did. In addition to his elephantine military spending, Reagan created the Department of Veterans Affairs, a whole new cabinet department (source:

U.S. Department of Veterans Affairs). Reagan developed a job training program, starting in 1982 (which I think was one of the few positive things he did for those in need). He spent billions of dollars on the Strategic Defense Initiative (also known as "Star Wars"), an anti-missile system to be stationed in outer space using lasers to destroy incoming Soviet weapons, which never got off the ground (source: www.u-s-history.com).

"By 1985, after billions of dollars but minimal results, Reagan's SDI was shut down but research continued," the www.u-s-history.com web site states. This program, started in 1983, has cost the American public $209 billion, up to 2013 (source: allgov.com, 5/26/2013. Allgov is a non-partisan news site that produces news articles on Federal and state government activities).

Reagan also re-started development of the B-1 aircraft program, which had been canceled under President Carter. The program cost $28 billion, and the airplane did not perform as expected in terms of its ability to jam enemy radar. The New York Times called the plane a "$28 billion turkey" (source: NYT, 7/17/1988).

He paid for all this stuff that didn't work on the nation's credit card. Reagan's policies remind me of Wimpy, from the old Popeye cartoons from the 1930s (I used to watch them on TV in our basement in the 1960s): "I shall gladly pay Tuesday for a hamburger today." Except Wimpy never paid. Reagan never paid either. (Where is Popeye when you need him? Probably looking for a can of much-needed spinach.)

Here's the thing. Reagan proposed that tax cuts for the rich would give them more money to invest and spend, which would create more jobs. He also said the tax cuts would pay for themselves, with more revenue coming back to the Federal government.

It didn't happen.

Reagan was the leader in bringing consumer culture to government. He promised a lot (tax cuts will increase government revenue), but delivered the exact opposite of what he said the cuts would do, just like corporations do all the time. The American people bought into his vision, but we have ended up paying and paying again for the fakery he promulgated.

Reagan offered a wonderful dream with the folksy smile of your Uncle Fred, selling us a brand new idea about tax cuts, but delivered the exact opposite of what he said the cuts would do. Rich people got more money. The poor and middle class got screwed.

That alone should be enough to discredit tax cuts for the rich, but conservatives keep throwing out tax cuts for the rich as a policy idea and Republican Presidential candidates keep talking about it, despite the fact that tax cuts have been proven to do nothing but give the rich more money and more power.

The wealthy have thoroughly embraced the major message of a consumer culture that tells us we should all get more for ourselves. Nothing else matters. As Margaret Thatcher, Great Britain's Prime Minister during the Reagan years, said, "…there's no such thing as society. There are individual men and women and there are families."

This is a perfect illustration of the ethics of consumer culture. And it's one of the worst things any country's leader has ever said, and I'm including Adolf Hitler in this evaluation.

How can you lead a country, which has a government designed to represent the millions living within designated borders, with a long and notable history, common customs and laws created to treat everyone equally and say such a stupendously ridiculous thing?

Why have a nation at all if you don't believe in society? Everyone in a country needs to take the other into account. If you could drive through red lights at will, without taking into account the people in "society," you could hurt and kill someone else. If you hit someone else and hurt them, shouldn't you be punished? Without society, there is just the law of all against all. So, take that Margaret Thatcher!

But the Reagan income tax cuts remained, and the debt and the deficit grew. And here's the thing. Reagan cut taxes for the wealthy, but raised them too, with the middle class and poor taking proportionally bigger hits than the rich. He increased gas taxes by a nickel a gallon. He increased taxes on Social Security.

"For many middle- and low-income families, this tax increase more than undid any gains from Reagan's income tax cuts of 1981...Thanks to President Reagan, those with moderately high earnings see their payroll taxes rise every single year," states libertytree.com, written by an anonymous, former member of the Republican Party until the presidency of George W. Bush.

Also, and more importantly, Reagan's tax cuts were, in effect, a transfer of wealth from the Federal government to wealthy people. With the Federal government running deficits, the Feds had to buy more bonds to finance the massive deficits the Reagan tax cuts caused.

"...if government spending is greater than tax collections, the result is a deficit. The federal government then must borrow money to fund its deficit spending," states the National Priorities Project (NPP), a non-partisan organization that tracks the Federal budget.

"To finance the debt, the U.S. Treasury sells bonds and other types of securities," the NPP says.

Who buys the bonds? Wealthy financial institutions and corporations. Who pays interest on the bonds sold? The American people. So, all of us, in society, pay to subsidize income tax cuts for the rich. We are the ones who are accountable for their consumption.

After Bill Clinton somehow managed to balance the budget and pay down our enormous debt, by raising taxes on the wealthy, then making budget-cutting deals with a Republican Congress (a Democrat did this, people), George W. Bush took a whack at tax cuts again and we were left off in much worse financial shape.

Bush the Younger demonstrated that he knew how to spend money on all kinds of stuff without the means to pay for it.

He expanded Medicaid by allowing seniors to buy prescription drugs under the program, called Medicare Part D. The program would have no cost containment provision. In other words, the Federal government would be unable to negotiate any senior drug prices downward.

Bruce Bartlett, who worked in both the Reagan and Bush the Elder's administrations, condemned W. and the

Republican Congress who passed this bill into law with these words:

"...Republicans refused to raise the Medicare tax or cut spending to cover Part D. Hence the deficit increased by virtually the entire cost of the program...Through 2012, Medicare Part D added $318 billion to the national debt (see 'General Revenue' on page 111 in the 2013 Medicare trustees report). That same report projects that Medicare Part D will add $852 billion to the debt over the next 10 years" (source: economix.blogs/nytimes.com, 11/19/2013).

Bartlett continues by writing: "The record also shows that such 'deficit hawks' as the current House speaker, John Boehner of Ohio; the current House majority leader, Eric Cantor of Virginia; and the current House Budget Committee chairman, Paul Ryan of Wisconsin, voted for Medicare Part D all the way." Ryan succeeded Boehner as Speaker of the House in 2015.

Why did Bush do it? The 2004 election was coming up and Bush thought the election would be close. Bartlett says Bush wanted to improve his share of the senior vote.

The strategy worked. Bush improved his share of the senior vote and won the election. The American people have to pay for his extravagance. Here again, is consumerism, George W. Bush style. He wanted to buy an election and he did. But he didn't pay. We pay.

Then we have Bush's merry little Iraq war – Operation Iraqi Freedom. This disaster of a war has cost us at least $820 billion (source: Frontline/PBS.org). The Bush Administration claimed the war would cost no more than $60 billion. Bush and his people sold the American people on the idea that we had to take out Saddam Hussein because he had weapons of mass destruction. Bush also linked Saddam with the 9/11 attacks, which further fed the hunger of Americans ready to take revenge.

"In his prime-time press conference last week, which focused almost solely on Iraq, President Bush mentioned Sept. 11 eight times," stated a 3/14/2003 article in the Christian Science Monitor. "He referred to Saddam Hussein many more times than that, often in the same breath with Sept. 11…Bush never pinned blame for the attacks directly on the Iraqi president. Still, the overall effect was to reinforce an impression that persists among much of the American public: that the Iraqi dictator did play a direct role in the attacks…"

"…the White House appears to be encouraging this false impression, as it seeks to maintain American support for a possible war against Iraq…'The administration has succeeded in creating a sense that there is some connection [between Sept. 11 and Saddam Hussein], says

Steven Kull, director of the Program on International Policy Attitudes (PIPA) at the University of Maryland," the article states.

It was an excellent sales job, but the problem is that the seller also bought this twisted vision.

Bush sold himself a bill of goods. He seemed to have grand visions of finding huge caches of weapons of mass destruction, getting revenge for 9/11, liberating the country and bringing freedom to the Middle East. Here is yet another case of someone buying into a beautiful dream which turns into ashes.

I refer you to George Packer's excellent book, "The Assassin's Gate – America in Iraq," for a full accounting of the selling of the war and the delusions of the Bush Administration, which turned into a nightmare for our soldiers and our nation.

In the midst of going to war in Iraq, Bush and a Republican Congress implemented a tax cut that I can only describe as bigger than Godzilla. The overwhelming share of the tax cuts went to the wealthiest Americans.

The tax cuts achieved the following:
- The very top one tenth of one percent of the highest earning Americans, who earn more than $3 million a year received an average tax cut of

$520,000. "That is over 450 times the tax cut received by an average middle-class family," stated The Campaign for America's Future, a progressive think tank, on its web site, citing the Economic Policy Institute's research.

- People making between $40,000 and $70,000 received less than an 11 percent share of the Bush tax cuts.

- Those bringing in less than $20,000 got about a 1 percent share of the tax cuts. "Seventy-five percent of these low-income families saw no tax benefit at all, The Campaign for America's Future said.

The Bush tax cuts destroyed the budget surplus Bill Clinton had worked so hard to achieve.

"In January 2001...the Congressional Budget Office (CBO) projected a ten-year surplus of $5.6 trillion...By comparison... (the Bush tax cuts) will reduce revenues by $1.35 trillion between 2001 and 2011," according to the Brookings Institution, a Washington think tank, in a June, 2002 report.

Packer quotes Joe Biden, a U.S. Senator at the time, as saying, "How urgent can this be if I tell you this is a great crisis, and at the time we're marching to war, I give the single largest tax cut in the history of the United States of America?"

Packer then goes on to write: "The tax cuts didn't just leave the country fiscally unsound during wartime; their inequity was bad for morale. But the president's failure to call for shared, equal sacrifice wasn't accidental. It followed directly from the governing spirit of the modern conservative movement that his presidency brought to full power. After years of a sustained assault on the idea of collective action, there was no ideological foundation left on which Bush could have stood and asked what Americans could do for their country."

This is the kernel of the problem. We have been taught for more than 30 years that there is no common purpose – just selfish indulgence of our own needs and wants, by corporations and the conservative movement, which has controlled the Federal government for two-thirds of this time.

And it's no accident that we were sold these policies by Reagan and little Bush, men who smile easily and personably and seem like they would be better company than those too-serious Democrats. They were great sales men. They promised us great things. They told us they were going to help us. We swallowed their personal and simple appeals.

Reagan changed the mind-set of Americans when he said during the 1980, "Are you better off than you were four years ago?"

Everybody wants to make more money. We need income to support our families and create a good future for our children and ourselves. However, Reagan's rhetoric reduced our vision from a national project to that of a household.

Let's contrast this brilliant conservative shrinkage of the election debate into a tiny box about family finances with a President from 20 years earlier.

John F. Kennedy famously said in his Inaugural Address, "Ask not what your country can do for you. Ask what you can do for your country."

I was about six years old when President Kennedy was assassinated. In my elementary school, I read those words in a biography of Kennedy. I didn't really understand them at the time. I was mainly interested in playing with my toys.

But now, looking back on those words, we as a nation may want to remind ourselves of what President Kennedy said and what it means.

With the lamp of history, we can view President Kennedy as a tremendously flawed individual and leader. Despite all his many transgressions, I believe there is still something powerful in Kennedy's words. The President was asking us to think of something greater than ourselves. He was asking the citizens of this great country to come together and do things together with a common purpose to improve the nation's and humankind's lot.

Kennedy's call was the exact opposite of the siren call of consumerism. There are many times where it seems the rich and powerful have turned their backs on their fellow Americans. They do not answer JFK's request to go beyond their own narrow self-interest.

Instead, the rich have seemed to turn inward. They want tax cuts and more tax cuts. They want to make themselves even richer than they already are. There are plenty of politicians in the Republican Party who keep wanting to help give them the candy they think they deserve.

The candidate for President from the Republican Party in 2016, Donald Trump, attempted to focus the election debate in terms of security. He did not talk about tax cuts in his convention address accepting the nomination of the party. But he put them out there.

This is another case of Republicans putting out the candy dish on the table for you while filching money from your back pocket. To borrow a line from President Reagan in another context, if a Republican proposes a tax cut for you, watch your wallet.

Trump's tax cuts could make interest rates skyrocket and push the national debt into the stratosphere.

"Donald's Trump's tax and spending plan could nearly triple interest rates and increase the federal government's debt by $14 trillion by 2026, according to an estimate by Mark Zandi...at Moody's Analytics" (a financial analysis firm), reported the Christian Science Monitor in its June 22, 2016 edition.

Zandi's investigation of Trump's plan revealed that "In 2018, the federal government could be paying more than $900 billion in interest – nearly twice what it pays today. By 2026, it could be paying more than $1.8 trillion in debt service, 50 percent more than under current fiscal policy."

Not only that. Zandi predicted that Trump's economic policy would cause a recession. Also, the plan would cause government deficits, government borrowing and interest rates to scream upward

"By 2026, Treasury would be paying $1.8 trillion in interest on its debt, one-third more than under current law...Interest would become the federal government's single biggest expense, 2.5 times spending for national defense, $550 billion more than Medicare and $200 billion more than Social Security. Interest payments would consume 6.7 percent of the nation's total economic output, and one quarter of all government spending," The Christian Science Monitor (CSM) article explained.

The higher interest rates that are anticipated will cause families to pay out more in interest for their homes, cars or any significant purchase than they would receive in tax cuts, the CSM article concluded.

Who really wins with Trump's tax plan? The rich will. They are the primary holders of bonds. They will earn interest on those bonds. Here again is a plan that will transfer money to the wealthy by taking it away from the poor and middle class.

Trump and his businesses have gone into bankruptcy four times (source: ABC News, 4/21/2011). Let's hope that Trump doesn't do the same to the country, under the guise of yet another screwball Republican plan to try to hand you what he claims is free money. It's a fraudulent trick that plays to consumer desires for an easy buck.

Consuming the Environment

We are eating the planet.

It's not pretty.

In Canada, in the province of Alberta, nearly 50 companies, including Exxon Mobil, Conoco Phillips, Koch Resources LLC, Chevron and Enbridge, have torn apart 140,000 square kilometers of forest and wetlands. This is almost the size of the state of Florida, which is 170,000 square kilometers (source: visualcapitalist.com, 9/1/2014), in order to dig out from the ground the dirtiest oil found on Earth.

If you look at before and after photos of what the oil companies have done, go to betterhomestead.com, as I did. The before photo shows a land ripe with trees and streams, a real magic kingdom of nature, as opposed to the Disney kind.

The after photo is a vivid illustration of nature's death. The trees are gone. The land has been scraped of all greenery. It is a vast black, grey and brown plain, with no life.

One machine used to perform the feat of removing the soil in the tar sands region was the RH400, a three-story-high hydraulic shovel, which scooped up 9,000 tons of earth in just an hour (source: Popular Mechanics).

Go to the betterhomstead.com website, look at the photos and tell me that digging up this land is worth the cost in oil. You can't.

It is estimated that between 11 million and 47 million tons of carbon pollution will be released by tar sands mining (source: the globeandmail.com, 3/11/2012).

"Before tar sands companies arrived on the scene, peatland fens comprised at least fifty percent and possibly as much as two-thirds of the region's boreal landscape," stated Canadian writer and photographer Ed Struzik in an 3/27/2014 article on e360.yale.edu, a publication of Yale University's School of Forestry and Environmental Studies. A fen is a type of wetland.

"These fens supported a wide range of plants, including many of western Canada's wild and rarest orchids; hundreds of species of birds; untold number of insect species; as well as a range of large mammals, including woodland caribou, moose, wolves, and grizzly bears."

That's all gone now.

The tar sands industry is using vast quantities of fresh water to mine the tar sands. Ed Struzik wrote in another article for Yale in 2013 about the amount of water the companies are taking to mine the tar sands for oil.

"In 2011, companies…siphoned approximately 370 million cubic meters of water… which was heated or converted into steam to separate the viscous oil, or bitumen, from sand formations. That quantity exceeds the amount of water that the city of Toronto, with a population of 2.8 million people, uses annually," Struzik wrote.

Also, and I love this, the companies are paying zero for the water. They are using a common resource to mine their oil. Essentially, the provincial government of Alberta is subsidizing the mining of the tar sands by charging nothing for the water they use.

"Nor do they clean it after recycling it and pumping it back into underground aquifers or into tailings ponds, which now cover 170 square kilometers – 66 square miles," Struzik wrote. (This is about the area of two islands of Manhattan – source: visualcapitalist.com). The water used becomes so toxic, that it's stored in these tailing ponds, which leak, because they are made of sand (source: www.Care2.com).

Struzik quotes a freshwater scientist and lawyer, William Donahue, on what we ought to call environmental theft on an immense scale.

"Nowhere in the world are we seeing this amount of groundwater being used for industrial development," Donahue said. "The scale of these withdrawals is massive and totally unsustainable."

In conclusion, the oil companies are completely tearing apart a northern forest and wetlands, destroying habitat for all kinds of animals, from birds to bears, taking city-size quantities of water from a beautiful river, polluting aquifers with toxic water and leaving behind a wasteland of black and brown muck, all to burn oil that "produces three times more greenhouse gas emissions than a barrel of conventional oil" (source: desmog.blog.com).

This insanity will increasingly heat up the planet, yet it is being done to fuel our industrial economy and make huge profits for the corporations involved.

China, the world's leading emitter of greenhouse gases, is also the world's leading coal miner (source: World Coal Association).

Here's a fact that should send a chill through anyone reading this: Not only is it the world's largest producer of this black, burnable rock, it's the world's largest consumer of coal, and "many of China's large coal reserves have yet to be developed" (source: M Bendi Information Services).

China burns as much coal as the rest of the world combined (source: MIT Technology Review, 5/27/2015).

"...giant coal mines of the interior (of China) have ravaged thousands of square miles," the MIT Technology Review article stated.

When I looked on the web, for photos of China's coal mines, I found pictures with the same type of brown, black and grey wasteland I found when I looked at Canada's tar sands sites.

China's coal mining and processing and coal chemical operations are polluting the country's Yellow River, which supplies drinking water to 50 cities and irrigation for the country's farmers (source: Greenpeace.org). The country converts much of the coal to oil and gas. The factories use water to process the coal, then dump it into the Yellow River. A photograph on Greenpeace's web site shows about a dozen plants, lined up along the Yellow River, spewing carbon pollution into the air.

China is now a materialist culture, modeled on the achievements of the United States. The government wants to provide its people with a rising standard of living, to become like the West. China wants to be like us.

On one hand, I can say, who am I to begrudge them their aspirations? On the other, I have to ask about the costs involved, to all of us. Even the U.S. may not be able to maintain its standard of living if the environment continues to deteriorate.

The U.S. is second to China in coal mining and India is third. A photo of the Powder River basin in Wyoming, where coal is mined, reveals a landscape where no trees or crops will grow and no human or animal could survive. The Powder River basin is the leading coal producer in the U.S. and provides 40 percent of the nation's coal (source: Wyoming Mining Association [WMA]).

Here's how coal mining works in Wyoming, according to the WMA: "Before the coal can be removed from the ground, the topsoil and dirt above it is removed using scrapers."

The soil is removed. What nature put in place over millions of years can be wiped out very quickly. Scrapers are giant machines with drills, shovels and giant draglines. Some of them have buckets that can move "160 cubic yards of material in one scoop," according to heavyequipment.com, an industry web site.

One cubic yard of topsoil weighs about one ton, or about 2,000 pounds (source: American Topsoil, a company that sells soil for gardening). Clearly, something that can move 160 cubic yards of soil in one scoop is a monster of a machine. One earth moving machine I found on the

Popular Mechanics website is a coal excavator that is 310 feet tall and 722 feet long. Nature isn't going to last very long with this thing around.

Following are some more hard facts that should scare the crap out of you, from the WMA:

"Each person in the U.S. uses 20 pounds of coal every day and 8 out of 10 tons of coal are used to produce electricity...Coal is also widely used in U.S. industries and manufacturing plants to make chemicals, paper, ceramics, and a variety of metal products. It is an important source of coke for the steel industry, and coal by-products are used to make linoleum, medication, detergent, perfumes, food flavorings, fungicides, insecticides, solvents and wood preservatives."

Would I prefer to have a fancy new kitchen table or food to eat?

Our choices may come down to simply that.

As of June, 2016, approximately 7.4 billion humans, plus uncounted animals and insects, need and share Earth's atmosphere. If we continue to heat it up with carbon pollution, we will imperil our ability to grow food. Global warming can cause land to dry out and become desert. It will increase heat waves and melt polar ice, increasing sea levels and possibly flooding our coastal cities. Life will become even more miserable for millions, and possibly billions who already live in poverty. How will we all get enough food?

No one, not even wealthy people, will necessarily be immune. For instance, David Koch, with a net worth of $55 billion (source: therichest.com), and one of our biggest carbon polluters, a major investor in the Canadian tar sands travesty, who has spent tens of millions funding groups that actively deny and fight action against climate change, has a beach estate in the Hamptons on Long Island. I wonder how he will feel about climate change if his vast estate gets inundated by a rising ocean?

The European Union, closest in living standards and politics to the United States, also has big carbon pollution problems. Poland, still burning coal like the wicked witch on fire, has the most polluted air on the Continent (source: npr.org, 4/11/2015). Almost 85 percent of Poland's electricity came from coal in 2012. By 2030, about 75 percent of Poland's energy will still come from coal (source: Wikipedia.org).

Poland's economy was predicted to grow by about three and a half percent in 2016, according to the World Economic Forum. That kind of growth is not going to dissuade Poland from cutting its burning of coal for electricity.

Germany, with Europe's largest economy, is building coal plants. More than 40 percent of Germany's energy comes from coal. Also, the United States and other countries are shipping coal to Germany so Germany can burn it for their economy (source: phys.org,7/28/2014). In 2015, Germany cut a deal with its dirtiest coal-fired plants to stay in business until 2021 (source: Bloomberg.com, 7/2/2015). Is it a coincidence that the country's carbon emissions rose by 10 million tons from 2014 to 2015 (source: www.climatechangenews.com, 3/14/2016)?

Germany is going to act in a turtle-like fashion in ending its use of coal. "The government is considering plans to end coal burning by 2040 or 2050. In January, energy minister Sigmar Gabriel called for patience. He told a conference, in remarks...`When one considers the future of coal, I would urge that you do so less from an ideological standpoint and to think more about the economic consequences,'" the Climate Change News article reported.

Again, we see how short-term economic considerations are favored over the long-term consequences of climate change. I would also argue with Mr. Gabriel that climate change is not ideological. It is a scientific fact and it has arrived. It will increasingly affect us, our children, our grandchildren and on through the generations to come. Nature is going to having the last word on the fate of humanity.

Here are the scientific facts, from the European Environment Agency (EEA). These facts are quoted directly from the EEA's web site page of 11/19/2012:

- The last decade (2002 – 2011) was the warmest on record in Europe.
- Heat waves have increased in frequency and length, causing tens of thousands of deaths over the last decade.
- While precipitation is decreasing in southern regions, it is increasing in northern Europe...These trends are projected to continue.
- Climate change is projected to increase river flooding.
- The Arctic is warming faster than other regions. Record low sea ice was observed in the Arctic in 2007, 2011 and 2012.
- Melting of the Greenland ice sheet has doubled since the 1990s.
- Glaciers in the Alps have lost approximately two thirds of their volume since 1850 and these trends are projected to continue.
- Sea levels are rising, raising the risk of coastal flooding during storm events.

I did not see any ideology in these findings. I ask Mr. Gabriel to conduct an investigation into the ideology behind the scientific data iterated above.

India is the fastest growing major economy in the world (source: Center for Climate and Energy Solutions/C2ES). About 40 percent of its energy use comes from coal, about 22 percent comes from petroleum, with natural gas usage close to seven percent).

India is striving to almost double coal mining and production by 2020 (source: U.S. Energy Information Administration). Looking at the situation from the outside, an observer might well conclude that this is an awful idea. But coal is cheap and India has been among the many developing countries who say the United States industrialized with coal and we should be able to do the same thing. India's government has stated that it must use more energy to move more of its people out of poverty (source: Reuters.com, 3/12/2007.

What will be the cost to India?

"The boost in coal usage will also lead to rising carbon dioxide emissions, with the Indian subcontinent likely to be one of the regions worst hit by global warming," explained the 2007 Reuters.com article.

India's capital, New Delhi, has air that may be the dirtiest in the world, worse even than Beijing (source: New York Times, 2/14/2015).

"India's high vulnerability and exposure to climate change will slow its economic growth, impact health and development, make poverty reduction more difficult and erode food security," according to the U.N. Intergovernmental Panel on Climate Change (IPCC).

A June, 2013, World Bank report on climate change and India stated, "Under four degrees centigrade warming, the west coast and southern India are projected to shift to new, high-temperature climatic regimes with significant impacts on agriculture."

Let's chew over that phrase "significant impacts on agriculture" for a minute. The World Bank is saying that India is creating a situation in the future that may harm its ability to feed its own people.

With only a two-degree centigrade increase in temperature (centigrade and Celsius are essentially interchangeable), this is what could happen to the country, the World Bank report states:

"Seasonal water scarcity, rising temperatures and intrusion of sea water" (from rising seas) "would threaten crop yields, jeopardizing the country's food security...Should current trends persist, substantial yield reductions in both rice and wheat can be expected in the near and medium term...Under two-degree centigrade warming by the 2050s, the country may need to import more than twice the amount of food-grain than would be required without climate change."

The report continues by painting a nightmare scenario for the population of India, particularly the poor.

"Climate change is expected to have major health impacts in India – increasing malnutrition and related health disorders such as child stunting – with the poor likely to be affected most severely. Child stunting is projected to increase by 35 percent by 2050 compared to a scenario without climate change...Malaria and other vector-borne diseases, along with diarrheal infections which are a major cause of child mortality, are likely to spread into areas where colder temperatures had previously limited transmission... Heat waves are likely to result in a very substantial rise in mortality and death, and injuries from extreme weather events are likely to increase."

Here is the promise of India's economic development using fossil fuels more than negated by climate change. What good is it to "develop" economically if you vastly diminish the ability of the nation to feed its own people?

Japan was the fifth largest emitter of greenhouse gases in 2011, after India (source: Union of Concerned Scientists).

We don't usually hear about Japan and climate change, but Japan emits a great deal of carbon. Japan's emissions have been rising, because the country replaced its nuclear power plants with coal fired power plants (source: 7/17/2015).

Japan has pledged to cut its carbon emissions by more than 25 percent, but it also plans to build more than 50 new coal plants (source: carbonbrief.org).

It's hard to understand this contradiction in light of the effects of climate change that may well come Japan's way:

"Japan, in particular, the report (from the Intergovernmental Panel on Climate Change/IPCC) says, is likely to experience more frequent heatwaves, more intense rain and stronger typhoons, which could have drastic effects on public health, water, agriculture and wildlife...rice yields could decrease by up to 30 to 40 percent in central and southern Japan," stated natureasia.com, a science news web site.

Japan is willing to continue to power its industrial engines with coal at the risk of cutting its food supplies. Brilliant!

Australia, a heavy coal user and coal exporter, increased its carbon emissions from 2014 to 2015 (source: The Guardian, a British newspaper, in its 12/26/2015 online edition). The Australian government released its emissions report on Christmas Eve, The Guardian reported. Interesting timing.

"Coal burning is the main source of electricity in Australia," reported Cool Australia, a local environmental group. "Every day we burn the oil equivalent of 50 million barrels' worth of coal," the Cool Australia web site explained.

Also, the Australian government gives its coal companies $2 billion a year in subsidies. Sound familiar?

On the other side of the globe, countries with territory in the Amazon basin, the biggest rainforest in the world, are cutting it away (source: rainforests.mongabay.com, an environmental and science news and information web site). Those responsible are Peru, Ecuador, Bolivia, Colombia and Brazil.

These countries are cutting down their forests for gold mining, oil drilling, highway building, logging, cattle ranching, constructing and maintaining soy and palm oil plantations and dam building.

"Since 1978, over 750,000 square kilometers (289,000 square miles) of Amazon rainforest have been destroyed," mongabay.com reported on 1/23/2016.

"Deforestation also drives climate change," National Geographic points out on its web site. "Forest soils are moist, but without protection from sun-blocking tree cover they quickly dry out. Trees also help perpetuate the water cycle by returning water vapor back into the atmosphere. Without trees to fill these roles, any former forest lands can quickly become barren deserts."

I wish someone would point this out to the people cutting down the forests in South America, and in fact, all over the world.

"Removing trees deprives the forest of portions of its canopy, which blocks the sun's rays during the day and holds in heat at night. This disruption leads to more extreme temperature swings that can be harmful to plants and animals," the National Geographic site explains.

"Trees also play a critical role in absorbing the greenhouse gases that fuel global warming," National Geographic says. "Fewer forests means larger amounts of greenhouse gases entering the atmosphere – and increased speed and severity of global warming."

This is all true, and yet, from a moral point of view, it's extremely difficult for the United States and other developed countries to scold the Amazon countries for this wide-scale destruction. We did it.

Indonesia is doing it too. They are systematically killing their rainforest, as mentioned earlier in the discussion about Doritos and palm oil.

What is all this damage doing to the country? Climate change isn't some distant prospect for Indonesia. It has arrived.

"Shifting weather patterns have made it increasingly difficult for Indonesian farmers to decide when to plant their crops, and erratic droughts and rainfall has led to crop failures," explained the World Wildlife Fund's (WWF) 2007 report on climate change in Indonesia, as reported by globalgreenhousewarming.com, a web site covering climate change news.

"A recent study by a local research institute said that Indonesia had lost 300,000 tons of crop production every year between 1992-2000, three times the annual loss in the previous decade," the WWF report stated. It went on to conclude that "Climate change in Indonesia means millions of fishermen are also facing harsher weather conditions, while dwindling fish stocks affect their income. Indonesia's 40 million poor, including farmers and fishermen, will be the worst affected due to threats including rising sea levels, prolonged droughts and tropical cyclones."

"'As rainfall decreases during critical times of the year this translates into higher drought risk, consequently a decrease in crop yields, economic instability and drastically more undernourished people,' says Fitrian Ardiansyah, Director of WWF-Indonesia's Climate and Energy Program.

`This will undo Indonesia's progress against poverty and food insecurity.'"

Indonesia has permitted its palm oil industry to slash and burn its rainforest. It has changed the climate already.

"Indonesia's biggest risk exposure to climate change is perhaps the variability of rainfall and variations in the El Nino and La Nina weather conditions, which have changed the length of the dry and rainy seasons in Indonesia," said T. Nirarta Samadhi, the Indonesia country director for the World Resources Institute, in an email interview with the World Policy Review magazine, published 7/29/2016.

What Samadhi is saying in rather bland terms is that the country's rainfall patterns have changed, which will affect how much food the country can grow to feed its people.

If you talk to Russia, however, the government there thinks global warming might be a good thing.

Russia, the world's largest country by land area, might not exist were it not for its oil, gas and coal industries.

"We only think about drilling for more and more oil and selling it to the West, said Alexey Yablokov, a Russian environmentalist (source: thediplomat.com, an online news site dedicated to international affairs in Asia).

Russia's leader, strongman Vladimir Putin, has claimed that climate change caused by humans is a "fraud," the diplomat.com web site explained.

The reason is clear. Russia needs to sell more petroleum and coal to make money. The country has little else to offer the world besides fossil fuels.

In addition, Putin thinks the world might benefit from climate change. He thinks that warming would enable Russia to farm in land in the country's north, which is now mostly frozen. Also, climate change would allow Russia to more easily search for mineral deposits north of the Arctic Circle (source: diplomat.com).

Putin's nonchalant attitude about climate change may come back to bite Russia. Climate change could cause extreme "weather events" in the country's southern and western regions, such as drought, wildfires and changing river levels needed for irrigation.

As the diplomat.com news article said, for example, "In 2010, unprecedented summer heat caused massive wildfires that dramatically reduced agricultural output...destroying one third of the country's wheat harvest...The country experienced another major heat wave with a devastating impact on agricultural output in the summer of 2012...Accordingly, any gains in agricultural productivity farther north could be offset by drought and wildfire in southern and western Russian and by the effect of melting permafrost on the country's irrigation patterns, confounding any hopes of increased grain production."

Also, Russia's coasts would be subject to a rising ocean and erosion of the country's shorelines.

Putin is gambling that climate change is going to help his country, so he's not going to do much about it. He's going to keep the drills and spigots running for the foreseeable future. This is a terribly casual gamble he, and the world, may well lose. It's also the gamble of a man who's not willing to try to seriously develop Russia's other industries to any great degree, such as information technology. They seem to excel in cyber-espionage, particularly when it comes to the Democratic Party here in the United States (see: U.S. Election, 2016).

With all this fossil fuel burning and forest destruction, governments around the world bravely and with a straight face declared in Paris in 2016 they will cut their fossil fuel emissions so as to keep a global temperature below two degrees Celsius (source: Center for Climate and Energy Solutions). The European Union and 174 nations signed the agreement (source: United Nations newsroom). Even Russia, that rogue of rogues, signed it.

Reflecting on the Paris Accord, I can't help but think that the world's governments are making a choice similar to St.

Augustine, when he wrote: "Lord, make me chaste, but not yet!"

Based on what I've seen from fossil fuel companies and countries, it's going to be extremely hard for them, and us, to stop consuming our own environment. Digging up the planet and selling its energy sources makes too much money for people to care what it's doing to our world. The riches that can be gained are too compelling to make anybody really cut down, or actually stop mining our little blue and green world, the only one we know of that can create and sustain life.

At the same time, we're burning fossil fuels and putting carbon in the air, we're cutting down trees by the billions that can help absorb that carbon. I feel that I'm living in some kind of weird Twilight Zone world where fossil fuel fans think that destroying our world will somehow save it.

This is mindless consumerism at its worst. This point of view sees the Earth's resources as simply products that can be turned into other products. The only intrinsic value they have is monetary. Trees, soil, mountains, prairies, meadows, water, oceans, rivers are all just things we must use to power our economy, until they're exhausted. People have to get paid.

It's like the woolly mammoth. Man hunted the mammoth to extinction (source: Daily Mail, 6/5/2014). Then he found something else to kill. Well, we're running out of things to kill.

Our resource-extraction economy, which is justified by claiming that consumers are constantly demanding cheaper goods, better service and more convenience, is based on an ideology that says the only way we can improve our living standards is to trust the market, a subject I will address in the next chapter.

Consuming Ideology

William Simon, a former Secretary of the Treasury, under presidents Nixon and Ford, once wrote a book called, "A Time for Truth." The book was published in 1978. I read it in the late 1970s, when I was in college.

The signature quote from the book was this and it has stayed with me ever since:

"Let a free economy rip."

Implicit in what Simon wrote was the idea that if you simply take away the vast majority of intrusive and unnecessary regulations businesses operate under, every business would be wildly free to make deals, sell products and prosper. When that happens, businesses would hire many more people and anyone who wanted a job could get one. Everyone could enjoy the fruits of an economy growing like crazy and households would enjoy tremendous leaps in their standard of living.

This ideology is a standard element of the conservative movement package. The Cato Institute, a conservative think tank founded and funded by the Koch Brothers, billionaire free market advocates who deny climate change, whose business relies on burning as much carbon as possible and who want to privatize Social Security, education, our national parks and even water, has explained its philosophy on markets and regulation like this (source: Wikipedia.org):

"Science can inform individual preferences but cannot resolve environmental conflicts. Environmental goods and services, to the greatest extent possible, should be treated like other goods and services in the marketplace. People should be free to secure their preferences about the consumption of environmental goods such as clean air or clean water regardless of whether some scientists think such preferences are legitimate or not. Likewise, people should be free, to the greatest extent possible, to make decisions consistent with their own risk tolerances regardless of scientific or even public opinion."

I am going to try to break down and analyze this paragraph. I think the Cato Institute is saying that people are free to drink water that may be polluted and breathe dirty air, if they want to, regardless of whether this is healthy or not. They regard air and water as products that people can consume and don't need to be regulated. People can choose clean air or dirty air. They can choose clean water or dirty water. They can live near a petrochemical plant if they want to. They can mine coal, if they want to, and never mind the doctor who says you'll get black lung disease. Last, and most importantly, companies should be able to do whatever they want to the environment, because the environment is just part of a world marketplace of goods.

The Cato Institute argues that we need not pay attention to scientists who find that pollutants are harming us and condemn the poor health effects caused by pollution from any source. These arguments are all made in the name of greater individual liberty for all.

Their thinking seems to align quite nicely with that of Margaret Thatcher, who stated, "There is no such thing as society," whom I cited in an earlier chapter on government.

David Koch himself lives in Manhattan and the Hamptons on Long Island. He does not live near a coal power plant or an oil refinery or gold mine. Koch has determined that he wants to live in a nice environment, but the Cato Institute writer he employs is telling us we don't have to have the same environmental goods he has, because, you know, if we want to drink bad water or have our children breathe polluted air, that's our decision!

Here's the problem with free market ideology, which the Republican Party has clung to for at least four decades. When businesses use water, that's a common resource. When they pollute the air, they're polluting a common resource. We all need to breathe. We all need water. Businesses profit from the use of these resources, but don't often pay for their use and abuse. Corporations get the money, but society is left with the bill to clean up the mess they have made.

Why should we consider water and air consumer goods? They're essential for human and animal life. The Cato Institute would let businesses buy and sell these things as if they were products.

Although Republican Party candidate Donald Trump has said odious and racist things about Mexicans, Muslims and many other things during the Presidential race of 2016, Trump is fully in tune with Republican Party ideology on climate change. He doesn't believe that it is actually happening. He has said he thinks it's a hoax.

Trump and the Republican Party have swallowed whole the ideology that unregulated free markets can solve all our problems. For instance, if we sell off the national parks, the land can be developed for expensive homes in beautiful places. Or fossil fuel companies could use the former park to drill for more oil or coal. Wouldn't that be great?

The economic activity created by selling off the national parks would be a great spur to our economy, this ideology argues. And, let's face it, according to the Cato Institute, the American people don't actually own the parks, even though they pay taxes to support their maintenance.

(The Cato Institute says the American government owns one-third of the land in the country. I don't know if that's true, but the American government does own a lot of land, especially in the West. However, the American government is not an isolated actor. It represents the American people. It is holding the land in trust for its citizens.)

Those who can't afford to buy houses in the former national park system would be making a "choice" not to live in a nice place, but instead, perhaps in a run-down trailer or a housing project riddled with violent crime in the inner city. See, everyone's happy and free!

The ideology of free markets has blinded conservatives in the Republican Party to the dangers of climate change. They have a massive case of cognitive dissonance. They can't believe that climate change is in fact occurring because it's inconsistent with their ideology that free markets deliver the greatest goods for individuals.

Never mind the actual reality that government subsidizes businesses with money for the oil, gas, sugar and agricultural industries and in effect provide common resources such as air and water for free, while the profits go to a few people at the top.

The free market ideology conservatives believe and promulgate has helped to deliver climate change to the world. The U.S. government has actually done very little to combat climate change. Congress has never passed a bill regulating greenhouse gases. President Obama attempted to issue rules to help cut carbon pollution from power plants by almost a third by 2030, but even this small effort has been frozen due to a lawsuit by 24 states, electric utilities, including the Alabama Power Company (a large consumer of coal for its plants) and coal mining companies, such as Murray Energy (source: Scientific American, 4/12/2016).

The Scientific American article stated: "In the EPA's argument defending the plan, the agency calls carbon emissions from coal-fired power plants a `monumental threat to Americans' health and welfare' by causing climate change, which leads to rising seas, coastal flooding, threatened water supplies, the spread of infectious disease and more frequent extreme weather."

On the other side of the argument, allying with the EPA were: "California, New York, Illinois, Massachusetts and 14 other states plus the District of Columbia and the cities of New York, Los Angeles, Chicago, Philadelphia and South Miami," the Scientific American article reported. "They have expressed concern for the health of their residents and the long term viability of their economies...State officials say their communities are already experiencing sea level rise, increasingly severe storms and prolonged droughts because of climate change, and they fear these events will only get worse. They're counting on the EPA to regulate the carbon emissions that could submerge them beneath the ocean in the coming decades, they said."

Here we see the dichotomy between private interests and the public interest. According to the Koch Brothers and the Cato Institute, there really isn't any public interest. There are just individual economic actors.

Trump, during the Presidential campaign, pledged to scrap any regulations on oil, gas and coal burning, so America can be great again.

However, despite Trump's professed point of view that climate change is not occurring, his golf course operation in Ireland applied to the government there to build a sea wall to protect the club from rising seas and erosion due to climate change (source: politico.com, 5/23/2016).

Trump is allowed to protect his operation, like any business owner. But this move by his golf course betrayed a contradiction. Trump's company was saying climate change is going to harm his own private interests. But, for the rest of us? We'll be left to fend for ourselves. Because, you know, climate change is just a hoax.

We need to be clear-eyed about both capitalism and climate change and not let ourselves be consumed by an ideology that says free markets can solve everything.

They can't. Capitalism has wrought tremendous leaps in our standard of living. I don't want to plant my own crops. I don't want to labor as a farmer 24 hours a day. I enjoy electricity and using a computer. I'm glad a doctor can help me with any health problems our family suffers. I like having the time to read books. I like learning about physics and biology.

However, we also need to recognize that even though capitalism has given us many benefits in improving the way we live, it has also given us climate change. We need to act to prevent the most extreme scenarios of climate change from falling around our ears.

Already, we see the evidence of climate change in various hot spots around the world. Global temperatures have been rising every year since the early 1960s (source: climate.nasa.gov).

Nasa.gov stated that the 10 warmest years since records have been kept "have occurred since 2000, with the exception of 1998."

Also, "The year 2015 ranks as the warmest on record" (source: NASA/GISS). "This research is broadly consistent with similar constructions prepared by the Climatic Research Unit and the National Oceanic and Atmospheric Administration," the NASA web site said.

California has suffered from increasing wildfires and massive, multi-year droughts. The Western U.S. has seen entire forests of trees die off from heat. Greenland's glaciers lost one trillion tons of ice in the years 2011 to 2014 (source: Geophysical Research Letters). Both the North and South Poles are losing ice at an increasing rate (source: NASA). Rising seas threaten our coastal cities (source: climatecentral.org).

After college and two years of working in journalism, I went into the private sector. I worked for a corporate training company and a series of public relations agencies for almost 20 years. I learned how hard it can be to make money. The companies I worked for had to do a great job providing great service to our corporate customers. We had to pay the bills, pay the workers, pay taxes, and earn a profit in a highly competitive business environment. We also had to follow government work rules and regulations.

I understand that business executives feel that government regulations are annoying, intrusive and possibly unnecessary. I don't agree with them, because the government is built to help protect people in cases where business won't, which, unfortunately, is a lot of the time.

When Al-Qaeda destroyed the Twin Towers, who was there to help? When Hurricane Sandy hit New York and

New Jersey in 2011, who was there? When central Oklahoma was laid waste by tornadoes and storms in 2013, who was there? When West Virginia suffered torrential rains and floods in 2016, who was there?

The government of the United States of America.

Businesses have a responsibility to their shareholders and their employees (I hope). But, despite what the Cato Institute thinks, the world is full of common resources we all share and which we need to live. Corporations don't seem so keen on helping us preserve the environment we depend on for our lives, from ExxonMobil and Alabama Power to PepsiCo and Coca-Cola.

If the business world isn't going to care for the environment, then who is going to help protect us from extreme climate change? There's only one answer.

I don't want to live in a world where I have to buy fresh, unpolluted air and carry it on a tank on my back. I don't want to live in a world where I have to buy the clean water I drink from the tap. I don't want to live in a world where we need to build giant, air-conditioned tents over our cities and towns so we can walk outside.

What happens if the Earth grows too hot to grow food? Are we going to have to rely on private companies to make synthetic food? How expensive will this food be? Are we all going to end up eating protein packs made of plastic pellets because while there may not be any food, there always seems to be plenty of plastic to go around?

The biggest obstacle preventing the United States government from working to prevent an extreme climate disaster being visited upon us all because of an undiluted consumerist drive to dig up and use ever more fossil fuels is the Republican Party and its enormously influential allies in the coal, oil and gas industries.

The ideology that unregulated free markets can solve all our problems needs to die if we are going to figure out some way to prevent climate change from cooking the planet beyond habitability.

Questions and More Questions

I'm not going to sit here and tell you I somehow, amazingly have a solution to the problems caused by consumer culture, from extreme selfishness to climate change. I can't even get my daughter to listen to me when it's time to go to bed (Well, really, I can, but it takes a lot of effort).

I do have some suggestions that might help, however.

First, we all need to start looking around and ask fundamental questions about how we live and how we can change our lifestyles in order to help preserve the planet.

We can start buying more fuel-efficient, hybrid, biodiesel and electric cars and cut consumer use of gasoline. We can replace the use of coal or natural gas to power our homes by buying wind power, which is what our family does in our apartment. It's becoming easier to purchase solar power. Also, we can buy smaller homes that don't use so much energy.

Consumer culture encourages us to believe that only our individual needs matter and that our needs must be instantly met. We must fervently reject this ethic, because it has created a diseased culture that leaves us unable to solve our most pressing problem – how will we stop the climate from changing into something currently unrecognizable to humans and therefore end our existence?

From consuming endless tons of tortilla chips, soda, guns, gas, coal and oil, we need to stop thinking only of ourselves. Many people I've met in my career seem to act like consumer zombies. They talk about what they want to buy or what they watched on television the night before. Their lives seem to have no overarching meaning.

Some people find that meaning in religion. I'm suggesting that we channel our need for meaning into saving our planet, so it remains a place where we can still grow healthy food, have plenty of clean water to drink and find a nice, soft, cool breeze to enjoy under the shade of a tree.

On the level of personal consumption, we can stop buying plastic water bottles and use bottles that can be used again and again. We can recycle our aluminum cans more. We can stop buying so much plastic. We can and should use canvas bags at the store instead of plastic.

We can boycott the companies who emit the most carbon pollution. Stop buying their products.

For instance, Chevron and Exxon Mobil were found to be the biggest emitters of greenhouse gases in the world over the years 1854 to 2010 (source: link.springer.com). Royal

Dutch Shell and Conoco Phillips were ranked sixth and ninth on the list, respectively. Peabody Energy, an American company which declared bankruptcy in 2016, is on the list as well. Consol Energy, also an American company, mines coal and produces natural gas.

The rest of the companies are foreign, and out of our reach, including Saudi Aramco, BP, Gazprom (Russia), the National Iranian Oil Company, Pemex (Mexico), Petroleos de Venezuela, Coal India, Total France, Petro China, Kuwait Petroleum Corp., Abu Dhabi NOC, BHP Billiton (Australia), which mines coal, copper, iron ore and uranium, and Anglo-American (United Kingdom), a coal and metals mining company.

For a complete list of companies that have historically emitted the most carbon, go to: link.springer.com/article/10.1007/s10584-013-0986-y.

Boycotting the purchase of products from carbon polluters selling their foul junk in America is one way you can stop helping them pollute the air with carbon. Make a statement that you don't support what they're doing. Buying Exxon, Chevron, BP and Shell gasoline and oil signals that you like their products. Vote with your feet. Don't buy the gasoline and other products they make that they sell directly to consumers.

Also, Wal-Mart is one of the biggest users of coal-fired electricity in the country (source: www.commondreams.org). In 2014, Wal-Mart emitted more than eight million metric tons of carbon into the air every year. If Wal-Mart were a state in the union, it would burn more than 34 other states. The company burns as much coal as New York and California combined (source: fusion.net).

The company gives lots of money to politicians who support fossil fuel energy (source: Institute for Local Self Reliance). So when you buy from Wal-Mart, you are supporting its fossil fuel usage and helping to warm the atmosphere. Plus, you're almost certainly supporting politicians who deny climate change and block any meaningful national and state legislation to stop it.

As an enormous retail chain, Wal-Mart is tremendously vulnerable to a boycott of its stores. Stop buying from Wal-Mart and let them know on their Facebook page or corporate website why you're not going to shop at their stores anymore. Write an article for your local newspaper or online news web site on how you won't shop at Wal-Mart until they stop using coal for electricity and switch to renewable energy.

PepsiCo, a consumer goods giant, should be similarly vulnerable. Tell the company you won't buy any of their

Doritos until they stop cutting down the rainforest in Indonesia.

Shout out your boycott on social media. Post on Facebook and Snapchat that you will no longer buy Wal-Mart, PepsiCo, Exxon, Chevron, Shell or BP products, all with stores and outlets in the U.S.

You can also announce the conversion of your electricity consumption from coal and natural gas to wind and solar on social media. You just might help persuade others to do the same.

Another important thing we can do is push for developing more environmental education curricula in schools. Students from the first grade through college need to learn more about what climate change is and how to stop it from accelerating. They also need to learn what they can do on a personal level, that change begins with all of us.

We can plant trees whenever and wherever possible. We can help preserve the land instead of digging it up for more homes or pipelines or drilling projects.

There are many non-profit organizations who will perform these tasks. American Forests plants trees. The Nature Conservancy and The Trust for Public Land buy land and preserve it. Conservation International buys land as well, overseas, to preserve it as wild.

The Environmental Defense Fund is trying to increase the use of clean energy sources and lower methane emissions from natural gas drilling, and working with China to decrease its carbon pollution emissions, among its many other projects.

The Natural Resources Defense Council is working to limit power plant pollution and make our cars and our homes more energy efficient and fighting to keep lands wild in their natural state.

The Union of Concerned Scientists promotes the use of clean, renewable energy, urges us to stop using coal and promotes sustainable agricultural practices.

There are many more groups out there, such as the Moms Clean Air Force, the National Audubon Society, the Rainforest Action Network, the Rainforest Alliance, the Wildlife Conservation Society, the World Wildlife Fund, the Ocean Conservancy and Earthjustice. Help them with their work. Give them money to fight against Big Coal and Big Oil.

Beyond the personal level, we all need to become a pain in the neck. We need to lobby, loudly, for our state and federal politicians to pass legislation to cut our manic consumption of fossil fuels and prevent extreme climate change from degrading our planet to the point of no return. We need to talk to our relatives (who may watch Fox News) about the need to switch their electricity from coal and natural gas to solar or wind power. This is becoming easier by the day.

If you really want to make a difference and you have the energy, join 350.org and work with them to act against the drivers of climate change. 350.org is an international organization, with a presence in 188 countries, aggressively moving to fight against the use of fossil fuels.

350.org, with support from local groups, helped stop construction of a coal plant in the Philippines in 2015. They helped stop the construction of the Keystone pipeline, which would bring tar sands oil from Canada to the U.S. The organization works to pressure governments and universities and individual investors to divest their shareholdings in fossil fuel companies. The city of Berlin voted in June, 2016 to divest their pension fund holdings in oil, gas and coal companies, joining Paris, Oslo, Copenhagen and Stockholm (source: 350.org). They will train people as local activists and help you start your own group to fight climate change.

Beyond this, run for office. Talk about climate change. Show people that we don't have to live and die with fossil fuels.

You can start small. Run for your town or city council. Look for ways the town government can reduce its use of fossil fuels and how to make town buildings more energy efficient. You can show people how to save money on energy bills. Plant trees on the front lawn of the municipal building. Use vacant lots to plant community gardens, so people can grow fruits and vegetables locally. Sponsor farmers' markets to promote the purchase of food grown in the area. Partner with local environmental groups on recycling metal cans and plastic bottles people throw on the ground or in local streams and rivers.

Mahatma Gandhi said: "If we could change ourselves, the tendencies in the world would also change. As a man changes his own nature, so does the attitude of the world change towards him...We need not wait to see what others do."

Martin Luther King said, "The arc of the moral universe is long, but it bends towards justice."

I would like to believe that. To make what Dr. King said a reality, we need to push ourselves to do more. There is no justice in fossil fuels. It pollutes the air with toxic materials that can cause all kinds of diseases and cancers. It warms our planet. It is all being done in the name of consumption. We need to call out the fossil fuel companies on their perilous activities and stop consuming their products.

Consumer culture has helped foster in us a sense that only our needs and wants are of predominant urgency and all that matters is satisfying those needs and wants right now, without any regard for the future consequences of our actions.

We must push back against this culture of crassly dangerous individualism. We need more spiritual sustenance than Coca-Cola, Doritos and a fully loaded SUV the size of a tank.

Fight for a bigger world than the pinched, self-centered dreams the consumer companies are selling you. We need a moral purpose. Fighting the use of fossil fuels around the world can give us that moral purpose. Life should not be based on you just filling your body with junk food, video game thrills and trucks that are big and fast.

Today, we must question everything about our lives. Are we just consuming machines who live to buy? Should we allow ourselves to be herded into a cut-rate discount store to find the best deals on televisions? Is this who we are?

This country, this America, was founded on a powerful, new idea -- that people should be free to pursue their lives, work and spiritual fulfillment in a way they decided for themselves.

But, isn't it possible that we have today, in a sense, given away our freedom to choose how we live? We let powerful, global corporations choose things for us. We're allowing them to tell us what's cool, what's manly, what's feminine, what's satisfying, what's worth buying. We're giving them the power to feed us exaggerations and lies.

And we're buying their stuff. We do that a lot. Too often, what we buy isn't really satisfying us.

On a personal level, I don't like buying a lot of stuff, but that's my own taste. I don't have the right to tell you what to buy, except when it affects my right to live, which is what's happening today. We're buying all kinds of things that are laying waste to our air, water and soil.

Perhaps consumer culture wouldn't be so consequential if all we get is more goods. But the consumer system we live in is digging up the planet, burning the atmosphere with heat and leaving us poorer in health and in spirit. We have the right to get fat, but does that mean it's a good idea?

There has got to be more to life than getting and spending and feeding our cravings, particularly because consumer culture relies on fossil fuels to deliver goods to our door.

Consumer culture has a big giant hole in the middle of its message. Because it is built on selling goods and services to satisfy needs, wants and illusory excitements, consumerism has nothing to truly nourish the soul. There is a great emptiness to it.

We all need to spend more time thinking about our place in the universe. It's not intuitive to us because we can't feel it, but we should consider these facts. We are traveling at 67,000 miles per hour on a giant round rock spinning around a star 93 million miles away. Traveling at the speed of light, it takes eight minutes for the sun's rays to reach us, giving us the energy all living things need to survive.

Our nearest planetary neighbors do not appear to harbor any type of life whatsoever. The temperature on Venus right now is about 800 degrees Fahrenheit (426 degrees Celsius). The average temperature on Mars is about minus 80 degrees Fahrenheit (minus 60 Celsius).

As for the rest of the planets in our solar system, at this point they appear to be barren of life. It is possible that certain moons orbiting Jupiter and Saturn may have liquid water and some form of life, but we have not yet discovered that life.

We beam out messages looking for life on other planets in our universe. So far, we have not found anything. Maybe, someday, we will.

But for now, the people and animals on Earth are the only life we know of in the universe. This extraordinary fact means that we have a responsibility beyond drinking our next Coca-Cola, doing battle in an Internet video game or getting a Botox injection to preserve the life that has arisen here.

If we die out, if the animals die out, because of our folly, then something important will be lost – a consciousness on the planet and in the universe.

When I was a much younger man, I read two books by Lewis Thomas. One was "The Lives of a Cell: Notes of a Biology Watcher." The other was "The Fragile Species." He was a medical doctor and professor, researcher and scientist, teacher and philosopher.

In his book, "The Lives of a Cell," Thomas wrote: "The oldest, easiest to swallow idea was that the earth was man's personal property, a combination of garden, zoo, bank vault, and energy source, placed at our disposal to be consumed, ornamented, or pulled apart as we wished."

Too many of us still believe this hoary, old idea. We should not be here to pillage the planet, because its resources are not infinite. We are nightmarishly capable of killing the world.

We need to be good stewards of this Earth, not barbarian hordes ravaging everything we find.

Again, I rely on the wisdom of Dr. Thomas, who wrote: "Statistically, the probability of any one of us being here is so small that the mere fact of our existence should keep us all in a state of contented dazzlement."

Well, most of us do not do this. I wouldn't expect too many people think about it. However, Dr. Thomas' thoughts are worth contemplating in light of our ongoing destruction of our biosphere, the complex set of living structures upon which we depend.

Our atmosphere is a thin film stretched around the planet, which keeps us warm from the frozen blackness of space, and which supplies us with the air we need for our bodies to function and survive. It extends about 62 miles, or 100 kilometers from the surface of the Earth (source: The International Aeronautical Federation). If the distance from one point on the ground to space were laid flat in a single line you could drive it in an hour.

The air we breathe is the product of the abundance of plant life which uses water and the sun's energy to survive and reproduce. It should trouble us greatly that we are cutting down about 60,000 square kilometers each year, about the size of Ireland (source: Rainforest Action Network/RAN. We destroy all these trees at our peril.

Listen to Dr. Thomas again: "...the life of the planet began the long, slow process of modulating and regulating the physical conditions of the planet. The oxygen in today's atmosphere is almost entirely the result of photosynthetic living, which had its start with the appearance of blue-green algae among the microorganisms."

We are here because of plants and trees. We all need to do a hell of a lot more to make sure they stick around, for our own survival, if nothing else.

We cannot keep chopping down trees and plants to make way for new Wal-Marts and Exxon Mobil gas stations and tar sands oil and coal mining. We can no longer afford to pave paradise and put up a parking lot. We will kill our home.

We cannot let Taylor Swift tell us to care about nothing more than romance. We cannot let Kanye West keep selling us expensive shoes, as if that were the most important thing in the world. We cannot let PepsiCo cut down rainforests for snack food.

We cannot let coal companies tell us we need coal to power our electricity. We cannot let oil companies tell us we need more oil and natural gas for our cars and homes and industries. We have to be better than that. We have to stop listening and start thinking. We have to find ways to create an economy that isn't based on warming the air to the point where it destroys our ability to eat and breathe, because that is what is at stake here.

Dr. Thomas put our place in the universe in perspective: "As evolutionary time is measured, we have only just turned up and have hardly had time to catch breath, still marveling at our thumbs, still learning to use the brand-new gift of language. Being so young, we can be excused all sorts of folly and can permit ourselves the hope that someday, as a species, we will begin to grow up."

If ever there was a time for us to grow up, this is it.

Personal Notes

You may well ask, who am I write this book?

The short answer is I wrote this book out of personal conviction. I believe that we urgently need to face the dangers of climate change and act extremely quickly to solve this global disaster in the making. I also believe that consumer culture is preventing us from acting, because corporations inundate us daily with propaganda that says we should live for the moment and only care about ourselves without any degree of thought for the greater world beyond our eyes and hands.

The longer answer is that I have come to this position because of the journey I have taken in life. In 1979, I got a bachelor's degree in political science from Binghamton University in upstate New York, without necessarily thinking I would go into politics as a career. Politics was just something I wanted to know about.

Without any job skills to speak of, the next year I went to journalism school at the University of Oregon. I decided I wanted to write for newspapers. My older brother was already there, getting a graduate degree. My best friend applied to a different graduate school at Oregon, and off we went to the West Coast. At Oregon, I obtained a second bachelor's degree and some direction for my life.

My first job out of college was at a small, weekly newspaper in rural Florida, owned by the Scripps-Howard chain. The town, called Jupiter, was on Florida's east coast. It had farms and dirt roads and trailers. It also had a lot of undeveloped land near its beaches, which real estate companies wanted to build on. Burt Reynolds, the actor from the "Smokey and the Bandit" and "The Longest Yard" movies, had established a dinner theater near the beach, and at the time it seemed fairly popular with residents and tourists.

I worked for this paper for a year, covering the police, town and regional governments, environmental issues, beach erosion, business development, dangerous roads, whatever the editor threw at me.

I had grown up on Long Island, in a suburb of New York City, and I was anxious to get to the city and work and live there. I figured I had a year of journalism experience and getting a job in the city would be no problem.

I learned very quickly that I was wrong. The people who interviewed me were very tough. One energy industry newspaper editor told me he wouldn't hire me for New York, but I could go work for him in Atlanta.

That didn't sound like much fun. I didn't want to go back to the South. The heat really bothered me, plus I wanted the excitements of New York City – from the Brooklyn

Bridge to Little Italy, from Chinatown to Greenwich Village. New York had brownstones and bagels. It had dark, little restaurants with gardens in the back and movie theaters all over the place. There was Broadway and off-Broadway, the Yankees, the Mets. There was great pizza and jazz joints. The streets pounded with people in a hurry. The whole city was an adrenaline rush.

I ended getting a job with a small marketing magazine in the sleepy suburb of Garden City, on Long Island, a few miles from where I grew up. I spent a little over a year there and found the job profoundly dissatisfying.

I tried once again to get a journalism job in New York City, but found nothing. I answered an advertisement in the New York Times for a writer and editor for a salesforce training company, got the job and just like that, I left journalism.

For three and a half years I wrote and edited training manuals for corporate salesforces, working out of a small office close to Grand Central Terminal. The companies were involved in oil refining, coffee and cola manufacturing, toothpaste, printing, abrasives (that's all kinds of sand paper – you have no idea how much sand paper you can use), health care, watch making, pharmaceuticals, motels, truck rentals and weight loss. I wrote manuals for training telemarketers and corporate salespeople alike.

I missed journalism, but I had convinced myself that there was no future for me in the trade. So I did what I thought was the next best thing. I got a job as a public relations writer.

Over 14 years, I worked in public relations for various large and small corporations. I started my career in public relations in Manhattan writing press releases for a Saudi-Arabian petro-chemical company, the majority of which was owned by the Saudi government. Six weeks into my work for this client, the king of Saudi Arabia called for the destruction of Israel. I asked to be taken off the account, which my bosses humanely agreed to.

I went on to work for clients in the plastics, industrial composites, defense technology, software, laptop computers, servers, and graphic arts materials businesses. I wrote articles promoting these companies and their products in industry magazines. I enjoyed writing and finding out about how these industries worked.

Along about the tenth year into my public relations career, something happened to me, physically (I herniated a disk in my back and it became a chronic injury) and psychologically. I began to think my job was very limiting in its scope. There was a certain something missing. In the business world, you are there to make a profit for your company. After a while, it felt deadening to my soul. Also, public relations agencies have a certain amount of frenzy to them. Everyone is running around at the office and babbling on the phone at the speed of sound, all to please their clients. It's easy to burn out. I started looking at the psycho-hyper people whipping around me, their hands in the air and flailing, panicking about the latest insane client request coming at the last minute and thinking, "What are these people doing? Why are they so excited? We're just talking about products."

This line of thinking eventually led back to me. I wondered what I was doing there, but I didn't know what to do with myself. I kept going to work, and sitting at my desk, even though I felt chilled to the bone with alienation. I cast about for something to do that would give me more meaning and purpose than what I had in the business world.

It's not the easiest thing in the world to remake yourself at the age of 44, but I managed to do it after a bit of a struggle, getting a master's degree in education from Adelphi University on Long Island. I became an elementary school teacher, teaching first graders how to begin to read and write, and do math. We also work on science concepts, such as growing plants and how animals live. We talk about what it means to live as a citizen in our classroom and the world – that we are not just isolated individuals, but connected to everyone else.

My students learn that what we do matters and that our actions have consequences. I talk to them about recycling and give them grade-appropriate books on the environment and why it matters in our lives, that it's not some separate thing from humanity, that we are part of nature, that we need it. I fervently hope with the greatest hope they learn this one core principle and become adults who can help us preserve this wonderful, life-giving blue-green Earth.

From my youngest years, I have been a student of this life. Maybe that's why I became a teacher. I have always wanted to know where we came from and what is our purpose here. So, even as a child, I dug into books.

First, it was comics, which gave me the illusion and thrill of the physical strength Captain America or Batman brought to any fight with a very bad guy. A visit to the store on the avenue in our neighborhood and I could experience what it meant to live a good life, by defending those being preyed upon with your very large and powerful fists.

Captain America meant the most to me, because, in the 1960s and 1970s, he was unambiguously great. He defended American values. To my 12-year old eyes and ears, he believed in the promise and freedom of this nation and he was willing to fight for it.

After some time, I figured out there were limits to what comics could teach you, so I moved on, to books on world history, politics, religion and fiction.

As an adult, I continued to dig into books and I started reading books on physics, biology, astronomy, and the origins of the universe and life. I read about Judaism, Christianity, Islam, Buddhism.

I became the kind of guy who, out with his college buddies at a bar, filled with clinking glasses, disco music and the roar of hundreds of flirtations occurring simultaneously around him, wondered what the hell he was doing there. I constantly wondered about my purpose in life. Why am I here? How did I get here? Where am I going?

It took me a very long time to figure out that I had to find my own purpose, that it would not necessarily be defined for me by some superior entity.

Teaching is part of my purpose and so is writing this book. I am not an environmental expert, or a journalist who can spend months or years on a book. I am writing as a citizen of the United States, who cares deeply about what happens to this country and the world. I have tried to produce a book that is readable and compelling, that persuades any of you reading this to act, forcefully, to save our environment.

We cannot afford to let ourselves be distracted by glittery little things that are thrown at us by giant corporations who care nothing for us except for how many dollars we can toss their way.

Donald Trump summed up consumer culture best when describing his own selling tactics: "I play to people's fantasies...That's why a little hyperbole never hurts. People want to believe that something is the biggest and the greatest and the most spectacular" (source: New York Times, 7/17/2016).

In a way all corporations try to pull this trick, to get us to buy their stuff. It's time we walked away from their sales pitches and focus on what's real and what's important.

We must take an evolutionary leap of the mind to become a species that can ensure our own survival, as well as our animal relatives.

I am doing what I can. As I mentioned earlier, I obtained wind energy for our apartment. I recycle constantly – in addition to paper, plastic bottles, metal cans I see lying around my neighborhood, discarded by careless consumers. In early August, 2016, I ran into my city councilman on the street and asked him if he could work on installing a recycling bin on the corner where all the high school kids gather after the bell rings, by Dunkin' Donuts, a Subway restaurant and a pizza place. His name is

Andy Cohen. He may have the same name as the producer of all those "Real Housewives" shows on Bravo, but he couldn't be more different. The Andy Cohen who sits on the New York City Council is a very good man who cares about his constiutents and I hope he gets this little project done. It might help the environment.

I have also given funds over the years to various environmental organizations, which I have mentioned in this book, including everyone from the Nature Conservancy, the Environmental Defense Fund, the Natural Resources Defense Council, American Forests, Conservation International, Earthjustice, Earth Works, The Trust for Public Land, Save the Redwoods League, the Rainforest Alliance, the Rainforest Action Network and the Adirondack Land Trust.

I also sign a lot of petitions online, just about every day, to call on politicians to do something about climate change and preserve our environment. I don't know if this is useful or not, but I hope so, somehow, that it helps make a small bit of difference.

One of the petitions I signed was started by a 13-year old girl, named Anna Lee Rain Yellowhammer. She was trying to stop a Texas-based oil company from building a crude oil pipeline on her tribe's land, near the Missouri River.

There are others, like her, such as Hallie Turner, also 13 years old, who brought a lawsuit to force the North Carolina state government to cut the state's carbon emissions by four percent each year until 2050 (source: The Weather Channel).

A teenage boy from Colorado, named Xiuhtezcatl Martinez, who, with 20 other kids, is currently suing the U.S. government in order to get the country to fight climate change (source: Vice News). This kid has been fighting climate change since he was six years old. He has spoken about climate change to the United Nations, three times. He is out there every day fighting for a decent climate future for his generation.

I am inspired by these young people and I hope you are too.

This book is part of me doing what I can to help the kids fight climate change. I know I need to do more. I hope you find it within yourself to do more too.

This planet needs saving.

Bronx, NY, September 2016